# The Role of Engineering
# in
# Sustainable Development

## Selected Readings and References
## for the Profession

A publication of the
American Association of Engineering Societies
and the
World Engineering Partnership for Sustainable Development

As it is the objective of AAES to be a forum for the free expression and interchange of ideas, the opinions, positions and research stated in its published works are those of the original researchers and authors and not by the fact of publication necessarily those of the American Association of Engineering Societies, Ind. or related bodies.

ISBN 0-87615-030-X

Additional copies of this publication may be obtained directly from the publisher:

AAES
1111 19th St. N.W., Suite 608
Washington, D.C. 20016 USA

telephone: (202) 296-2237
facsimile: (202) 966-3240

This book is dedicated to the memory of two engineering leaders, Murray Sweetman and Geoffrey Coates, in honor of their pioneering efforts to promote sustainable development throughout the engineering profession worldwide.

**Edited and compiled by Monica D. Ellis**
**Graphics by Heather L. Robertson**

Special appreciation to the AAES Task Force on Sustainable Development and its Chair, Albert A. Grant, for their contributions and guidance in the publication of this book.

This book is made possible, in part, by a contribution from the Global Environment and Technology Foundation and the American Association of Engineering Societies.

# The Role of Engineering
## in
## Sustainable Development

## Selected Readings and References for the Profession

## Table of Contents

"Sustainable development is a process of change in which the exploitation of resources, the direction of investments, the orientation of technical development, and institutional change are all in harmony and enhance both current and futurepotential to meet human needs and aspirations. . . .

Sustainable development... meets the needs of the present without compromising the ability of future generations to meet their own needs."

World Commission on Environment and Development
*Our Common Future*
1987


"We cannot risk the consequences of a future built on an unsustainable foundation. It is up to us — the engineers and stewards of sustainable development — to see that future generations receive their heritage."

Henry J. Hatch, P.E.
Former Chief, U.S. Army Corps of Engineers
*Accepting the Challenge of Sustainable Development*
1992

# INTRODUCTION

In the final years of the 20th century, our planet is entering an unprecedented era of explosive change: a new age in which a dominant social, economic, and environmental theme will be the quest for "sustainable development." As conceived by the 1987 World Commission on Environment and Development and confirmed at the 1992 U.N. Conference on Environment and Development, human civilization has crossed a historical divide where, to ensure our long-term survival, we must learn to "meet the needs of the present without compromising the ability of future generations to meet their own needs."

The American Association of Engineering Societies (AAES) is a multidisciplinary organization of engineering societies dedicated to advancing the knowledge, practice, and understanding of engineering in the public interest.

The World Engineering Partnership for Sustainable Development (WEPSD) is a global initiative dedicated to unifying the world engineering community to facilitate sustainable development. The primary objective of the WEPSD is to create a global network for all engineers through technical advice and information sharing, capacity building activities, research and development, and the demonstration, dissemination and adaptation of environmentally benign technologies.

Engineers will play a critical role in sustainable development, and must acquire the skills, knowledge, and information which are the stepping stones to a sustainable future.

This collection of papers and references on sustainable development is intended as a basic primer on the subject for all engineers and for those with an interest in engineering. It brings together in one publication a number of widely recognized key papers on engineering for sustainable development, along with several policy statements by major engineering organizations, and an extensive reading list on sustainable development.

It is our hope that this book will be widely read by practicing engineers and students of engineering, and that it will stimulate interest in and understanding of basic concepts of sustainable development, and encourage engineers to take their proper leadership role in meeting this global challenge.

Ernest L. Daman
1993 Chair
AAES Board of Directors

William Carroll
1993 Chair
WEPSD Board of Directors

# Sustainable Development Policies:
# Statements from the Engineering Profession

# Statement
## of the
## American Association of Engineering Societies
## on
## the Role of the Engineer in Sustainable Development

## Introduction

The concept of sustainable development has been defined as a form of development or progress "that meets the needs of the present without compromising the ability of future generations to meet their own needs."[1]

Engineers will play a critical role in sustainable development. The American Association of Engineering Societies (AAES), whose member organizations represent more than 800,000 members in the mainstream of engineering design, construction, management, research and education in the United States, recognizes and accepts this critical role and challenge. AAES will work with and through the World Engineering Partnership for Sustainable Development (WEPSD), and its own member societies, to promote public recognition and understanding of the need for sustainable development, and the policies and technology required to achieve a sustainable world for future generations.

This policy paper broadly defines the challenge of sustainable development, and identifies a set of action principles for engineers to meet this challenge. It also provides a basic framework for comment and discussion within the engineering community and with other disciplinary groups who have a role in sustainable development. Based on this dialogue, AAES plans to generate a series of detailed policy and position statements on the action principles identified in this paper.

## The Challenge

Population is growing, urbanization is expanding, and the current demand on natural resources is outstripping supply in the developed and developing world. Environment, technology, and economic development must therefore be seen as interdependent concepts in which industrial competitiveness and ecological sustainability will be addressed together as complementary aspects of a common goal. Thus, as perhaps the dominant economic, environmental and social issue of the 21st century, sustainable development embraces the inextricable linkage of continued socioeconomic development, technology transformation, population growth, and the perpetual integrity of the Earth's natural systems.

This approaching age signals an environment that will be highly complex, interdependent, and fluid; and this will have implications for all professions. Engineers, as agents for the implementation of change, along with other professionals need to be adaptable to this changing environment. These concerns require a new thinking about the nature of development and demand an expanded role for engineers as part of the decision-making process itself and as agents for change. In this role, engineers must become "facilitators of sustainable development", through the information they provide, the decisions that they make, and those that they influence.

Sustainable development requires finding new ways to do business and demands dramatic changes in the culture of engineering. Sustainable development requires doing more with less: less resources, less energy consumption, and less waste generation. It requires conceptually new manufacturing processes and equipment, expanding use of recyclable materials and the development of regenerative/recyclable products. Sustainability requires focus on upstream pollution prevention in preference to "end of the pipe" clean-up technologies. Sustainability requires approaches that incorporate much higher levels of resource efficiency in manufacturing and disposal of products. Because the continuation of current development and resource consumption trends may well foreclose opportunities for a sustainable future, we must greatly accelerate the implementation of new sustainable technologies and manufacturing processes.

## Action Principles for the Engineering Profession

The following guiding principles provide a conceptual framework for the implementation of sustainable development by the engineering profession, and a strategic direction for transformation of the ethics, education, and practice of all engineering professionals:

### • Engineer Engagement in Shaping Decisions

We must assume a more assertive and proactive role in defining and shaping a desirable future. We must be ready to answer hard questions such as — What new tools and processes must be developed? What must we do as individuals and organizations to achieve these developments? How should we set priorities for this work? If we do not meet this challenge, then we will be left behind in the decision making process that will influence the future shape of this world. Engineering for a sustainable future will require engineers to engage more actively in political, economic, technical and social discussions and processes to help set a new direction for the world and its development.

## • Sustainable Development Education for the Profession and the Public

As facilitators of sustainable development, engineers must acquire the skills, knowledge, and information which are the stepping stones to a sustainable future. The promotion of sustainable development demands that engineers cultivate an understanding of the environmental issues, problems, and, especially risks and potential impacts of everything we do. Engineering education must instill in its students an early respect and ethical awareness for sustainable development, including an understanding and appreciation of cultural and social characteristics and differences among various world communities. In addition, we must provide our students with the analytical tools to assess risks and impacts, to perform life cycle analysis, and the ability to solve technical problems, cognizant of and taking into consideration the economic, socio-political and environmental implications. Moreover, we must strive to educate all elements of society and promote universal adoption of a sustainable development ethic; particularly among private and public sector decision makers, developers, investors, and local, regional, national, and international governing bodies.

## • Integrated Systems Thinking and Synthesis

Synthesis is the combining of separate elements to form an integrated and complete coherent system. In planning for sustainable development, engineers need to examine fully and systematically the aggregate long-term consequences of decisions, in terms of both time and space, and the alternatives which may lead to more environmentally sustainable choices.

## • New Environmental-Economic Measures and Analysis

Engineers need to acquire more environmentally sensitive and responsive economic tools to integrate environmental and social conditions into market

5

economics. A market economy based on a free enterprise system affords the best opportunity to achieve that level of national and global economic development that must occur to support the needs of growing populations while achieving sustainability.

## • Sustainable Technologies and Processes

The creation of sustainable technologies and processes is perhaps THE most practical and readily available tool to achieve the sustainable integration of the environment and technology in the foreseeable future. Technology focused on sustainable development is a key to solving problems created in the past and to prevent new ones arising in the future. Engineers must work with others to adapt existing technologies and create and disseminate new technologies that will facilitate the practice of sustainable engineering and meet societal needs.

## • Expanded Multidisciplinary Partnerships

Achieving global sustainability is a critical task that requires the efforts of many disciplines. We must approach the challenges of sustainable development as partners sharing the problems and jointly arriving at sustainable solutions. Public/private partnerships which forge cooperative relationships and place the long term viability of technology in the mainstream of social policy and resource decision-making are a necessary precondition to building a viable future.

AAES will support and encourage the development and application of these principles to strengthen the knowledge and ability of the engineering profession in meeting the challenge of sustainable development.

---

[1]"Our Common Future," Report of the World Commission on Environment and Development, 1987.

Reprinted with the permission of the American Association of Engineering Societies.

## *About AAES:*

**The American Association of Engineering Societies** (AAES) is a multidisciplinary organization of engineering societies dedicated to advancing the knowledge, practice, and understanding of engineering in the public interest.

# Engineering for Sustainable Development
## by the
## World Engineering Partnership for Sustainable Development
## (WEPSD)

The World Engineering Partnership for Sustainable Development (WEPSD) is a global coalition of engineering organizations committed to long-term actions in support of sustainable development. Dedicated to unifying the world engineering community to encourage sustainable development practices, the WEPSD is an interdisciplinary partnership between the international engineering, applied science, and business communities.

## WEPSD Vision

*"Engineers will translate the dreams of humanity, traditional knowledge, and the concepts of science into action through the creative application of technology to achieve sustainable development. The ethics, education, and practices of the engineering profession will shape a sustainable future for all generations. To achieve this vision, the leadership of the world engineering community will join together in an integrated partnership to actively engage with all disciplines and decision makers to provide advice, leadership, and facilitation for our shared and sustainable world."*

Sustainable development is the dominant economic, environmental, and social issue of the 21st Century. Engineers, as problem solvers, are at the nexus of this sustainable development debate. They possess the technical expertise to insure that the most appropriate knowledge in natural, technological and social sciences is utilized to meet the needs and aspirations of society in a sustainable manner. Engineers are the *implementing* interface between science, decision making bodies, and society.

As acclaimed engineer and author Sam Florman notes: " We live in a technological age and if our society is to flourish, many of our leaders should be engineers, and many of our engineers should be leaders". The need for technical leadership is particularly crucial with regard to sustainable development.

Consider that:

• At present, more than 1.5 billion people in developing countries do not have access to clean water and 2 billion have no access to sanitation.

- One fifth of the world's population breathes air more poisonous than World Health Organization recommendations.

- In just six years, by the year 2,000, the urban population of the developing world will almost double in size that of the industrialized world.

- Today, it is not possible to find a sample of ocean water with no sign of the 20 billion tons of human waste added to this resource annually.

- Approximately 1 billion people in the world live on less than a dollar a day.

- To merely cope with current population trends, the world economy will need to be five times larger in 2050 than it is today.

## WEPSD History

To effectively address the challenges presented by sustainable development, the WEPSD was formed in 1992 through the combined efforts of the following global engineering organizations:

- **World Federation of Engineering Organizations (WFEO)** - WFEO is the largest global engineering organization representing approximately 10 million engineers in 80 countries.

- **International Federation of Consulting Engineers (FIDIC)** - FIDIC is comprised of national associations of consulting engineers in 50 countries. As such, FIDIC represents the majority of the world's consulting engineers.

- **International Union of Technical Associations (UATI)** - UATI represents a grouping of 26 international non-governmental technical associations in over 120 countries.

Collectively, the WEPSD represents 12 million engineers worldwide. This alliance identified the following critical issues:

- The need to unify the global engineering community, particularly around the issue of sustainability.

- The belief that the world engineering community has a <u>responsibility</u> to apply its technical expertise towards the implementation of sustainable development at the individual, corporate, and institutional levels.

- The need to cultivate and unify key relationships in the global environment and development community with sustainability serving as the central bridge linking various organizations and resources.

With the June 1992 Earth Summit conference in Rio de Janeiro as a catalyst, the WEPSD formed a unified position on sustainable development. Since that time, the WEPSD has engaged with world leaders, policy makers, scientists and engineers to inform the world community of its willingness to support sustainable development with the expertise of engineering professionals.

## WEPSD Mission

The WEPSD functions as a non-profit organization whose member associations include engineers from industry, private practice, universities, environmental non-governmental organizations, governments, and multilateral groups.

WEPSD's mission is:

- To assist and interact with all engineering organizations to promote sustainable human development.

- To develop constructive relationships with all other stakeholders having related goals.

- To propose and coordinate projects/programs that will facilitate sustainable development.

- To represent the interests of engineering organizations in influencing public and private decisions in order to create a sustainable future.

## WEPSD Goals - 1994

1) Create an effective global communications network with all engineers and engineering groups to provide leadership and practical content to the concept of sustainable development.

2) Create and maintain effective relationships with other major groups, professions and disciplines (stakeholders) that are involved in future development and environmental programs.

3) Develop and promote global ethics, long-term capacity-building programs and improve professional practices for engineers and others involved in development/environmental programs (including stakeholders and decision makers such as regulators, developers, financiers, leaders, etc.).

4) Develop and implement both short and long-range plans for projects/ programs to be initiated and coordinated by WEPSD (and/or to be carried out in collaboration with others).

5) Create a permanent self-funding organization that is capable of global networking to stimulate and coordinate sustainable development programs/ projects.

## WEPSD Priority Focus

The WEPSD focuses its initial work in the following areas:

- Develop sustainable planning processes.
- Develop and apply technological systems for sustainable development.
- Advance industrial ecology and sustainable productive systems.
- Focus information on implementing sustainable development; and
- Focus engineering ethics and education on sustainable development.

## 1994 WEPSD Priority Projects

In 1992, the WEPSD Board of Directors developed the following listing of projects for immediate action. These projects were recommended by various WEPSD advisors and members and were selected as they directly relate to and support the WEPSD vision and mission.

•   Establish an international senior engineering task force to advise all Nations on the preparation and implementation of their national Sustainable Development Plans.

•   Establish an engineering communications network to develop and share sustainable solutions to pressing real-life technical issues and engineering problems, especially in developing countries.

•   Establish a series of Regional Engineering Centers as complementary *components* of the integrated regional center concept being developed by the international development community.

• Facilitate the research, dialogue, and policy decisions necessary to define and establish effective measures for sustainable projects, programs, and processes. (*The Metrics of Sustainability*)

• Institute a recognition and awards program to raise awareness of the relative sustainability of international projects, programs, and processes.

• Support the establishment of sustainable engineering ethics in every Nation and professional organization and inform every engineer of these emerging responsibilities.

• Initiate an audit of the curricula of engineering universities in various countries to determine their contribution to sustainable human development.

• Develop a sustainable planning process to include manuals and training components.

• Identify and summarize current information on international "sustainable engineering" activities and share this information globally.

• Develop a sustainable engineering anthology for wide distribution which showcases methods and the importance of engineering for sustainability.

Reprinted with the permission of the World Engineering Partnership for Sustainable Development.

# World Federation of Engineering Organizations (WFEO)
## Code of Environmental Ethics for Engineers

**The WFEO COMMITTEE ON ENGINEERING AND ENVIRONMENT,** with a strong and clear belief that man's enjoyment and permanence on this planet will depend on the care and protection he provides to the environment, states the following principles.

**To All Engineers**

When you develop any professional activity:

1. Try with the best of your ability, courage, enthusiasm and dedication to obtain a superior technical achievement, which will contribute to and promote a healthy and agreeable surrounding for all men, in open spaces as well as indoors.

2. Strive to accomplish the beneficial objectives of your work with the lowest possible consumption of raw materials and energy and the lowest production of wastes and any kind of pollution.

3. Discuss in particular the consequences of your proposals and actions, direct or indirect, immediate or long term, upon the health of people, social equity and the local system of values.

4. Study thoroughly the environment that will be affected, assess all the impacts that might arise in the state, dynamics, and aesthetics of the ecosystems involved, urbanized or natural, as well as in the pertinent socio-economic systems, and select the best alternative for an environmentally sound and sustainable development.

5. Promote a clear understanding of the actions required to restore and, if possible, to improve the environment that may be disturbed, and include them in your proposals.

6. Reject any kind of commitment that involves unfair damages for human surroundings and nature, and negotiate the best possible social and political solution.

7. Be aware that the principles of ecosystemic interdependence, diversity maintenance, resource recovery, and interrelational harmony form the basis of our continued existence and that each of those bases poses a threshold of sustainability that should not be exceeded.

Always remember that war, greed, misery and ignorance, plus natural disasters and human induced pollution and destruction of resources, are the main causes of the progressive impairment of the environment and that you, as an active member of the engineering profession, deeply involved in the promotion of development, must use your talent, knowledge and imagination to assist society in removing those evils and improving the quality of life for all people.

Approved by the Committee on Engineering and Environment of the World Federation of Engineering Organizations, in the 6th Annual Plenary Session, New Delhi, November 5, 1985.

## The WFEO Havana Resolution

The General Assembly of the World Federation of Engineering Organizations (WFEO) recommends that each National Member of WFEO take the following steps to implement the engineering contribution to the global plan of action of Agenda 21, and the Declaration on Sustainable Development made by the 1991 WFEO General Assembly in Arusha:

1.   Establish a code of ethics which recognizes the new responsibilities of engineers for sustainable development.

2.   Promote the inclusion of principles and practice of sustainable development in the curriculum of engineering education and training.

3.   Establish a national committee on engineering and the environment as a focus for the development of policies on the role of engineers in sustainable development.

4.   Support and promote the establishment of centers for sustainable development and environmentally sustainable technologies linked together in a national network for the exchange of information and research.

5.   Seek to incorporate national engineering institutions, including universities, research institutes, professional societies, and academies of engineering, in the national network.

6.   Support and promote the establishment of regional centers and networks for sustainable development, and asks the WFEO Committee on Engineering and the Environment to generate information that will assist national members.

The Havana Resolution. Approved by the WFEO General Assembly, 1992, Havana Cuba.

Reprinted with the permission of the World Federation of Engineering Organizations.

*About WFEO:*

**The World Federation of Engineering Organizations** is the largest global engineering organization representing more than 80 countries and 10 million engineers. WFEO's purposes are to encourage the formation and activities of national and international associations of engineers; to facilitate the exchange of engineering information; and to foster engineering education and training.

# International Federation of Consulting Engineers (FIDIC) Environmental Policy Statement

There is a growing awareness that the earth cannot continue supporting increases in population and consumption. Mankind is threatening its own existence, in addition to that of many other forms of life, through global pollution and excessive consumption of limited resources.

Engineers have contributed to the quality of life through the provision of better water supplies and sanitation and by the development of natural resources, food, energy, and communication and transportation systems. These advancements have contributed to rapid population growth and environmental problems.

Consulting engineers accept the challenge of the endangered environment. Because of their professional training and background they have a particular role and obligation towards the protection of the environment. Engineers should provide leadership in achieving sustainable development — development that will meet the long term needs of future generations of all nations without causing major modification to the earth's ecosystems.

This role of the engineer should result in:

- careful evaluation of the environmental benefits and adverse impacts of proposed projects.
- conservation of energy.
- reduction in the use of non-renewable resources and increased reuse of materials.
- reduced waste production through improved industrial processes, better transportation and distribution systems, and recycling of waste products.
- sound agricultural and other land-management practices.
- restoration or improvement of damaged land, polluted water supplies and disturbed ecosystems.
- effective transfer of environmental knowledge and experience.

## Ethics and responsibilities

Worldwide steps are required to protect and improve our enviroment. The efforts must involve government, the public, and the private sector.

Consulting engineers are trained and experienced in handling complex problems. They should combine their traditional skills with broader applications of physics, chemistry, biology and other disciplines to lead interdisciplinary teams directed at achieving acceptable environmental solutions.

Observing a code of conduct is a fundamental part of the profession of a consulting engineer. The goals of consulting engineers should include a commitment to achieve sustainable development. Consulting engineers should give highest priority to the short term and long term welfare, health and safety of the community. They should consider regional, global and cumulative effects of projects in addition to local effects.

## General Actions

FIDIC recommends that each consulting engineer should:

- Keep informed on global environmental trends and issues.
- Discuss environmental problems with professionals from other disciplines.
- Provide information to clients, the public and government about environmental problems and how adverse effects can be minimized.
- Become involved in organizational activities, including assistance to governmental authorities, that promote the protection of the environment.
- Encourage and promote appropriate environmental laws and regulations.
- Actively support and participate in all forms of environmental education.
- Promote research and development relevant to protecting and improving the environment.

## Project Actions

FIDIC recommends that consulting engineers should:

- Recommend that environmental studies be performed as part of all relevant projects. Such studies will normally require a multidisciplinary approach.

- Evaluate the positive and negative environmental impacts of each project. This evaluation might be based on a preliminary review of available information or on the engineer's experience. They should evaluate the basic functions and purposes behind a project. They should suggest alternatives to their clients if environmental risks emerge.
- Develop improved approaches to environmental studies. Environmental effects should be considered early in the planning process. Studies should evaluate the long term consequences of environmental changes.
- Make clients aware that engineers can reduce but not always eliminate adverse environmental impacts. The legal and financial responsibilities of all parties should be clearly defined.
- Urge clients to prevent or minimize the adverse environmental effects of projects in all phases — initial planning, design, construction, commissioning, operating and decommissioning.
- Finally, take appropriate action, or even decline to be associated with a project, if the client is unwilling to support adequate efforts to evaluate the environmental issues or to mitigate environmental problems.

Reprinted with the permission of the International Federation of Consulting Engineers.

*About FIDIC:*

**The International Federation of Consulting Engineers (FIDIC)** represents the majority of the world's consulting engineers. FIDIC is comprised of national associations of consulting engineers in 50 countries.

# Environmental Principles for Engineers
## by
## The Institution of Engineers - Australia (IEAUST)
## National Committee on Environmental Engineering

These principles were developed by the IEAUST National Committee on Environmental Engineering through extensive consultation with professional bodies, industry, government, and academia.

●●● "The further development of civilization, the conservation and management of natural resources, and the improvement of the standards of living of mankind are greatly affected by the work of the engineer. For that work to be fully effective, it is necessary not only that engineers strive constantly to widen their knowledge and improve their skills, but also that the community be willing to recognize the integrity and trust the judgment of members of the *profession of engineering.*" *(IEAUST Code of Ethics)*

●●● Engineers, because of their professional role in society, have a particular obligation towards the integration of development and the environment, leading towards sustainable development.

●●● The following environmental principles complement the IEAUST's Code of Ethics and incorporate the concept of ecologically sustainable development, and the practice generally of environmentally responsible engineering.

●●● Statements and policies from the World Federation of Engineering Organizations (WFEO), and the International Federation of Consulting Engineers (FIDIC) have been incorporated in part in the following principles, thus reflecting international thinking.

### ENVIRONMENTAL PRINCIPLES

#### 1. Engineers Need to Develop and Promote a Sustainability Ethic, and:

1.1 Recognize that ecosystem interdependence and diversity form the basis for our continued existence.

1.2 Recognize the finite capacity of the environment to assimilate human-made changes.

1.3   Recognize the rights of future generations. No generation should increase its wealth to the detriment of others.

1.4   Promote a clear understanding of the actions required in engineering practice to improve, sustain, and restore the environment.

1.5   Promote the development of alternatives to the use of non-renewable resources.

1.6   Promote the wise use of non-renewable resources through waste minimization and recycling, wherever possible in engineering activities.

1.7   Strive to achieve the beneficial objectives of engineering work with the lowest possible consumption of raw materials and energy, and by adopting sustainable management practices.

**2.   Engineers Need to Recognize the Interdisciplinary Nature of Engineering, and:**

2.1   Recognize that the expertise required for carrying out a specific engineering activity may not be sufficient for judging the environmental implications of that activity.

2.2   Involve other environmentally-based disciplines in determining the environmental implications of engineering activities.

2.3   Recognize individual limitations in assessing environmental effects, and respect other professional opinions.

**3.   Engineers Should Practice Engineering in Accord with a Sustainability Ethic that Leads to Sustainable Development, and:**

3.1   Study thoroughly the environment that will be affected, assess all the impacts that may arise, and select the best alternative for an environmentally sound and sustainable project.

3.2   Urge clients or employers to incorporate environmental objectives into design criteria, and to prevent or minimize the adverse environmental effects of engineering activities.

3.3 Include consideration of environmental effects at all phases of planning and implementation of engineering activities.

3.4 Consider the consequences of all proposals and actions, direct or indirect, immediate or long term, upon cultural heritage, social stability, health of people, and equity.

3.5 Identify and act to minimize potential environmental effects of engineering activities.

3.6 Rigorously examine the basic functions and purposes behind a project to recognize options and alternatives to improve sustainability.

3.7 Inform clients that engineers can reduce but not always eliminate adverse environmental impacts without incurring increased costs. This does not imply that increasing the cost will solve all environmental problems.

3.8 Suggest alternatives to clients if the proposed engineering activity is likely to create unavoidable environmental risks.

3.9 Urge clients to incorporate monitoring of environmental change into projects, and to adjust operations as a result of monitoring.

3.10 Include costs and benefits relating to environmental quality and degradation in economic evaluations of engineering activities.

3.11 Recognize the rights of the community to be involved in project formulation and development and actively encourage such involvement.

**4. Engineers should Act with Integrity, Objectively and Ethically, Remembering their Responsibility to the Community, and:**

4.1 Recognize all actual, potential or perceived conflicts of interest in relation to engineering activities.

4.2 Recognize that compromising environmental quality or standards in engineering activities is an appropriate means of reducing cost. This approach may only achieve short term gains at the expense of long term sustainability.

20

4.3 Provide information to clients, employers, the public and government about ways of improving the sustainability of engineering activities.

4.4 Disclose environmental implications and external costs of engineering activities, taking into account the often inadequate and uncertain nature of environmental data.

4.5 Report on environmental issues with honesty and integrity.

4.6 Decline to be associated with engineering activities if the client or employer is unwilling to support adequate efforts to evaluate environmental issues or to mitigate environmental problems.

**5. Engineers Should Pursue and Encourage Professional Development, and:**

5.1 Keep informed on global environmental trends and issues.

5.2 Actively support and participate in environmental education.

5.3 Maintain dialogue about sustainable development with other professions.

5.4 Learn the skills necessary to develop active community participation in engineering activities.

5.5 Assist and advise other engineers where necessary in the application and use of the principles of sustainable development identified in this document.

Reprinted with the permission of the Institution of Engineers - Australia.

*About the Institution of Engineers - Australia:*

**The Institution of Engineers-Australia,** founded in 1919, is a professional association of more than 60,000 professional engineers, engineering technologists, and engineering associates. The Institution promotes and advances the science and practice of engineering, ensuring that the community is well served by its engineering resources and encourages the development of Australia's technological capacity in a way that maximizes its contribution to the economic growth of the nation.

# Readings
## on the
## Engineer's Role
## in Sustainable Development

# THE WORLD AFTER RIO
by
## Dr. Thomas F. Malone

For two weeks in June 1992, the population of the bustling city of Rio de Janeiro was swollen by more than 30,000 persons. Heads of state and leaders of private organizations around the globe had gathered to address profoundly complex issues central to the quality of life and to human development on the planet they share. I was among those who converged in Rio for the "Earth Summit," formally the United Nations Conference on Environment and Development (UNCED), and the parallel Global Forum sponsored by the nongovernmental organizations.

I was keenly aware that UNCED was far from the first major international gathering on environmental issues; 20 years earlier I had been privileged to attend a U.N. conference on the environment in Stockholm. It was clear that the central environmental issues defined at the Stockholm conference remained salient for two decades later. But the debate over the earth's future had been reshaped. The new ways of thinking and talking about our environmental dilemma that emerged from the Rio conference are important to understanding the problems, promise and opportunities facing scientists, educators and political leaders in the aftermath of UNCED.

Delegates to the Stockholm conference had a goal to which most citizens of the world would describe today - a vision of physically attractive, biologically healthy and productive environment. It has become clear, however, that this goal cannot be discussed in isolation. Our vision of environmental quality has broadened. Along with a healthy and productive natural environment, we must have human development. All people, in the present and in future generations, must have equitable access to the goods necessary to meet basic needs such as food, clothing, shelter and good health. All must share in those legitimate aspirations that give meaning to sheer existence: culture, education, leisure, and social interaction. Both the responsibilities and the opportunities for achieving human development while preserving environmental quality fall particularly on the makers of knowledge and the makers of policy. These new dimensions were explored at the seminal, interdisciplinary Forum on Global Change and the Human Prospect sponsored by Sigma Xi in November 1991.

## Two Worlds, One Earth

The world population, and the global capacity to transform natural resources into the goods and services that meet human needs and wants, are both

25

doubling every few decades. During the past century, population has grown four-fold and economic production 15-fold. Both growth rates impinge upon the life-support capacity of the global environment.

But there are sharp asymmetries in demography and in economics between the two groups that constituted the major blocs at the Earth Summit: the seven industrialized nations in the North and the 122 still-industrializing nations in the South. The North, with about one-fifth of the world's total population of five billion people, produces and consumes four-fifths of all goods and services each year. The South, with four-fifths of the world's people, produces and consumes only one-fifth. For every person added to the population of the North, 20 individuals are added in the South. For every dollar of economic growth per person in the South, 20 dollars accrue to each individual in the North. In the North, the stress on the environment comes from an energy - and technology - powered economy and high consumption (hence the concerns about green-house-gas-induce warming and stratospheric ozone depletion). In the South, it comes from population pressure and low consumption (resulting in deforestation, desertification, and soil deterioration). One-fourth of the people in the South exist in a condition of absolute and degrading poverty, inimical to human dignity.

The outlook for the 21st century is troubling. Even if population growth in the South and economic growth in the North are both constrained, the world population will more than double, and the global economy will increase nearly sixfold *(Figure 1)*. The world may be embarking on a grand experiment to

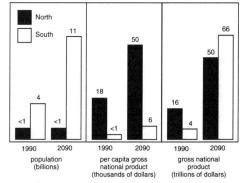

**Figure 1.** Current and projected population and economic contrasts between the industrialized nations of the North and industrializing nations of the South, based on assumed growth rates of 0 percent in population and 1 percent in per capita gross national product (GNP) in the North, and 1 percent in population and 2 percent in per capita GNP growth in the South. (Adapted from *World Development Report* 1991, World Bank and Oxford University Press.)

ascertain the limits to the life-support capacity of the biosphere. Estimates indicate that human activity uses, diverts or wastes 40 percent of the photosynthetic productivity on Planet Earth.

These circumstances suggest the need for four actions: stabilizing the world population, transforming the energy - and technology - powered economic system into one that is environmentally benign, reducing the economic and demographic asymmetry between North and South and, in particular, reducing absolute poverty wherever it is found.

These objectives were implicit rather than explicit in the deliberations in preparation for UNCED and in the documentation that emerged from it. The North came with a principle concern for global environmental issues. The South was preoccupied with economic development and poverty. The results of the Earth Summit reflect this dichotomy. That some common ground was found represents a triumph of international diplomacy.

**The Rio Agenda**

World consciousness was raised at the Stockholm conference in 1972. Modest but effective institutional innovations were made within the U.N. system and among participating nations, and the following years witnessed a slowdown, or reversal, of environmental deterioration in many countries - especially the United States. The role of science and technology in economic development was addressed at another U.N. conference in Vienna in 1979. That one foundered on the controversial New International Economic Order and on the failure of the North and the South to reach agreement on the level of financing for proposed programs.

Impetus for the Earth Summit was provided by the report *Our Common Future*, prepared by the independent World Commission on Environment and Development, and chaired by the Norwegian prime minister, Gro Brundtland. This report made a persuasive case that environmental quality and economic development are inextricably linked. *Our Common Future* held up the concept of "sustainable development" as a vision that would unite the North and the South in a common endeavor. This concept envisions an interplay of population growth, increasing economic production and consumption, and evolving technology in a manner that meets the basic needs and legitimate aspirations of the present generation without foreclosing options for future generations. In simplified terms, it means living on natural resource "interest," rather than drawing down natural resource "capital". Although somewhat ambiguous, the term "sustainable development" caught on and emerged as a central theme at the Earth Summit.

A period of intensive planning, discussion, negotiation, and compromise preceded UNCED, producing two major documents that constituted two major agenda items for the summit. They were the Rio Declaration on Environment and Development and Agenda 21.

The declaration constituted a set of 27 principles governing the rights, responsibilities and relationships of nations in the pursuit of sustainable development through "a new global partnership." Only muted reference was made to the reduction and elimination of "unsustainable patterns of production and consumption", the task of "eradicating poverty", the promotion of "appropriate demographic policies", and the "inherently destructive" nature of warfare. The declaration represented a compromise, fashioned mainly by Ambassador Tommy Koh of Singapore. A consensus could not be reached on a more ambitious and inspirational Earth Charter proposed during the planning period.

Agenda 21 is a document that may well serve as a blueprint for action. It is a several-hundred page strategic plan divided into 40 chapters, embracing 115 program areas to be pursued by the global partnership during the 21st century in the interest of sustainable development. It addresses issues as diverse as demographic pressure, agriculture, forests, fresh water resources, the atmosphere, the oceans, toxic chemicals, hazardous and radioactive waste, poverty, trade and technology cooperation. It contains proposals for institutional arrangements to ensure implementation of the activities recommended for each program area, and financial arrangements to underwrite their costs.

Primary responsibility for implementation will rest with sovereign states, although UNCED recommended the creation of a high-level U.N. Commission on Sustainable Development to coordinate international efforts toward that goal. Since it is clear that the South will require financial assistance in taking action on Agenda 21, a funding mechanism - the Global Environmental Facility - was proposed that would operate under the auspices of the World Bank, the U.N. Development Programme and the U.N. Environment Programme. International funding for Agenda 21 was estimated at $125 billion annually. About half of this amount would represent new money that might be obtained if nations (mostly in the North) increased the production of their gross national product that is now allocated to overseas development assistance to 0.7 percent by the year 2000. This was recognized as a desirable goal. The failure to obtain a firm commitment to this target was a distinct disappointment at Rio de Janeiro. The issue of financing is now under consideration at the 47th session of the U.N.

Various other topics on the UNCED agenda diverted public attention away from Agenda 21. The United States was at the center of controversy over conventions on climate change and biodiversity that were opened for signature at Rio. In both cases, the U.S.'s position isolated it from the other nations of the North. It is likely that residual reservations on both will be resolved in the negotiations that will transform conventions into treaties of historical significance. Deep concern by African countries over the issue of desertification led to a decision to recommend that a process be started that would lead to international negotiation of a convention for coping with this environmental phenomenon.

While the heads of state were working over tough policy issues, lively and informed discussions were underway at the Global Forum, which was attended by 20,000 representatives of non-governmental organizations. The debate at the forum included and went beyond the items on the UNCED agenda. Thirty-eight statements or treaties were drafted as a contribution to the deliberations initiated at the Earth Summit. Perhaps more important, informal networks were established that will provide a continuing mechanism for interaction within the non governmental community, and between that community and governments.

### A Bend in the Road

The significance of the Earth Summit is not found in the specific details of the programmatic and institutional recommendations it produced, in the blizzard of documents generated in the preparatory phase, nor in the controversy over draft conventions at Rio. It is found in the nature of the particular juncture in the continuing saga of humankind on Planet Earth that brought so many individuals (including 110 heads of state or government) to Rio to deliberate on the problems and opportunities that lie ahead during the first century of the third millennium.

In expanding the common view of our global dilemma to include the question of equitable human development, the Earth Summit represented a major step toward maturity in the consideration of the environmental *problematique* that has attracted increasing attention for the past two decades. The issues are daunting. The task is formidable. Both individual and collective responsibilities are substantial. However, avenues for solving problems and seizing opportunities exist. A major avenue is identifiable in the realization that knowledge is the driving force of human progress. It is knowledge about the world we inhabit and our place in that world that has brought us to this societal juncture. It is progress in the understanding of matter, energy, life processes and information, and their interactions, that has empowered individuals to transform the natural resources in the environment into the goods and services that satisfy basic needs and aspirations. The research community has been eminently successful in generating knowledge. Knowledge generation by individual investigators *must* continue; the need for new knowledge will only increase as societies advance. But greater emphasis, I believe, must now be given to integrating, disseminating and applying that knowledge.

Integration implies breaking new ground in interdisciplinary research and education at universities. Institutional reform and innovation to support these efforts will be necessary. Integration that crosses several domains of knowledge, such as the social sciences and the humanities, is mandatory.

Dissemination of knowledge touches deeply the role of education at all levels - informal as well as formal. A scientifically illiterate society is ill-prepared to make the kinds of decisions now required. The demographic and economic asymmetry between North and South is closely related to the knowledge of asymmetry. The urgent need to address this aspect of "capacity building" is often overshadowed by a preoccupation with technology transfer and financial "aid". New technology for information handling and interactive communications provides attractive opportunities for the scientific community to make a major contribution to this dimension of the knowledge issue.

Application involves forging new modes of global partnership among business and industry, governments, and the scholarly community. This is probably as crucial to the vitality of the research enterprises as it is to the fate of society. The coupling of knowledge generation and integration with policy formulation need not compromise the objective nor erode the standards of excellence that have been the hallmarks of the research community.

In addressing the central role of knowledge, it is useful to emphasize that the coupling of knowledge generation and integration with policy formulation will be most effective when pursued at the level where crucial decisions are made. In a highly diverse world society of sovereign nations, the optimal place is at a regional level. Proposals by the International Council of Scientific Unions and the Carnegie Commission on Science, Technology, and Government for regional networks are now being actively pursued. In the United States, an elevated role for individual states is indicated.

Since knowledge is the domain of the universities, that community has a splendid opportunity to articulate a declaration of principles, set forth a realistic vision of the world that science and technology can help to achieve and make a commitment to the innovations in education and research that will be necessary to realize that vision. The biblical injunction, "where there is no vision, the people perish", underscores a challenge to which the university community might appropriately respond.

The concept of sustainable development has been extraordinarily useful, but it suffers as a societal goal, for example, by not distinguishing between economic development and the emerging concept of human development. The latter embraces economic considerations but incorporates other essential human aspirations. It merits elaboration.

The opportunities for leadership are limitless. But these opportunities will be seized only if the individual members of the research community become informed and involved. An important step would be taken, in my view, were scientists to commit themselves to the notion of "tithing", in which each individual dedicates a portion of research time to becoming informed on human-development issues and to participation in policy-relevant or strategic research.

The most important contribution of the Earth Summit was its function as a catalyst for stimulating governments, business and industry, non-governmental organizations, individual scientists, and engineers to action. A framework now exists within which to begin addressing the issue of enhancing the quality of human life and human development everywhere on Planet Earth - now and in future centuries.

The outlines of a vision of that future are dimly visible: human development in an equitable society in a sustainable environment. The steps to achieve this vision are emerging. Many of them are found in Agenda 21. An urgent task is to focus on the overarching need to bring to bear on these societal problems the expanding storehouse of knowledge about the world in which we live, and human values and behavior in that world. The research community - its individual members and organizations - deeply committed to knowledge and intrinsically international in outlook, is in a position to exercise leadership.

**Bibliography**

Sigma Xi, The Scientific Research Society. 1992. *Global Change and the Human Prospect: Issues in Populations, Science, Technology, and Equity,* Forum Proceedings, Sigma Xi, The Scientific Research Society, Research Triangle Park, NC.

*International Environmental Research and Assessment: Proposals for Better Organization and Decision Making.* 1992. A Report of the Carnegie Commission on Science, Technology, and Government, Carnegie Corporation.

*Human Development Report, 1991.* U.N. Development Programme, Oxford University Press.

This article is reprinted with the permission of *American Scientist. Vol. 80, November-December 1992.*

*About the Author:*

**THOMAS F. MALONE**

Dr. Thomas Malone is a Distinguished University Scholar at North Carolina State University and Director of The Sigma Xi Center in Research Triangle Park, NC. His past positions have included MIT Professor, Foreign Secretary of the National Academy of Sciences, and President of the American Meteorological Society. Dr. Malone participated in the "Earth Summit" in Rio de Janeiro in 1992 as a special guest of Secretary General Maurice Strong and was appointed by the Executive Director of the UN Environment Programme to a 3 year term as a member of the Scientific Advisory Committee for the World Climate Impact Assessment and Response Strategies Program (WCIRP). He also holds a baccalaureate and a honorary doctoral degree in engineering from the South Dakota State School of Mines and Technology and is a member of the AAES International Committee.

# Accepting the Challenge of Sustainable Development
## by
## Henry J. Hatch, P.E.

*This article is adapted from a speech presented at the first meeting of the World Engineering Partnership of Sustainable Development, March, 1992, in New York City. It first appeared in Spring 1992 issue of the National Academy of Engineering's publication,* The Bridge.

A fundamental challenge faces the free world and all of us who are world engineer leaders — the challenge of achieving sustainable development. We must find a way to meet the needs of the present without compromising the ability of future generations to meet their own needs.

Sustainable development is the dominant economic, environmental, and social issue of the twenty-first century. The experience of the last 45 years proved to the world that we can achieve economic growth only through the synergy of pluralistic institutions and market economic systems. Now, more countries than ever are struggling to transform their political and economic systems. The ability of the global economy to grow could be limited by changes in our already stressed environment. The worst pressures are on the poor. World population will double sometime in the next century, and urban areas of the developing world will feel this increase acutely. By the year 2000, the developing countries will represent about 75 percent of the world's population. Economic expansion is a necessity. Failure to grow could result in regional conflicts. But economic growth without consideration of the natural resources, social conditions, and future generations is not long term, efficient, or effective. Unwise economic growth could also result in regional conflicts and threaten global security.

Engineers must play a critical role in the development of the future. We must accept the challenge.

**The Challenge**

The World Commission on Environment and Development has taken a leading role in outlining a sustainable future, culminating in the 1987 publication of *Our Common Future.* This report has provided a focused definition for the concept and impetus for action:

> *"...sustainable development is a process of change in which the exploitation of resources, the direction of investments, the orientation of technical development, and institutional change are all in harmony and enhance both current and future potential to meet human needs and aspirations."*

In other words, sustainable development "meets the needs of the present without compromising the ability of future generations to meet their own needs."

Sustainable development is finding new ways to do business. Sustainable development demands change. It requires doing more with less—less resource input and less waste generated. It requires new manufacturing processes, more use of recyclable materials, and the development of regenerative or recyclable output components. Instead of "end of pipe" technologies alone, it requires pollution prevention. Sustainable development requires that we consider the life-cycle consequences of production. It requires an approach that imitates natural or biological processes and seeks new levels of the resource efficiencies of production. Sustainable development challenges institutions to create new possibilities for the design of products and the use of natural resources. We must create new ways to market, produce, deliver, and dispose of products. We may need to develop new infrastructures or provide new services.

Sustainable development is not simple. There is no single blueprint. Countries differ in time and space. What works for developed countries may not work for developing or redeveloping countries. Many factors shape the possible options for each country. Factors can include social elements such as religion, background, market mechanisms, environmental resources, population, industrial structure, labor force, urban hierarchy, infrastructure, or geographic conditions.

How will sustainable development happen?

Engineers will translate science and the dreams of humanity into action to serve the objectives of sustainable development. We will apply technology—but in new ways. Through our ethics, education, and practices, we will shape a sustainable future. To achieve this vision, the leadership of the world engineering community is merging into a multidisciplinary partnership. We will actively engage with all disciplines and publics to provide advice, leadership, and facilitation for our shared and sustainable world.

A partnership is paramount to achieving a sustainable future. To be successful, sustainable development requires a "process" for change — first, knowledge, awareness, and understanding of the conditions for development, and, then, commitment to act. Effective decisions to invest in essential social, physical, and institutional infrastructure require understanding. That understanding is not only of what is going on, but the forces at work across cultures, oceans, and paradigms. Effective decisions to develop or adapt technologies require that same understanding. Critical to the process for change are the knowledge bases that describe the gamut of interactive physical, chemical, biological, and human processes that shape what is sustainable and what is not.

The process for change requires the expertise and responsibility of all disciplines in cooperation at all levels — global, regional, national, and local. While every society, and perhaps every individual, will ultimately become involved, the engineering profession must play a major role in implementing change. Engineers are the action agents for transformation and change. To maximize engineers' potential for success, we must actively engage with all disciplines and publics to start the process of change for a secure, stable, and sustainable world.

Engineers of the world have a significant role in designing and building a sustainable future. The engineers provide the bridges between science, society, and the public and private decision-making bodies. Engineers must take the lead in implementing the best available science and technologies to meet the needs of the present generations without foreclosing options to future generations. The engineers must focus on not only the whys but also the whats and the how tos. For example, how do we transfer technology to meet sustainable development objectives and the specific needs of a country? The engineers of the world must become more active in the political, economic, technical, and social discussions and processes of development. They must help to set the new direction.

Engineering for sustainable development demands profound attention to hard questions. To become effective partners, the engineering profession must adopt a new ethic and a new culture — a new way of thinking and acting. Engineers must accept that development — an improvement in the quality of life — can take place without causing an increase in the quantity of resources consumed. Whatever the discipline, the promotion of sustainable development demands that engineers cultivate an understanding of the issues, problems, and, especially, the risks and potential impacts associated with our daily decisions. This will happen through an expanded environmental and social education. We must approach sustainable development in a way that imitates the complexities of natural processes, a multidimensional, systemic process. Economic, cultural, environmental, and technological factors are all interdependent. This interdependence requires that the projects be examined for their impacts on the ecosystem.

The engineers of the world must take responsibility for translating concepts into action. This begins through the creative application of research. Creative application of technology encompasses the responsibility to plan, design, and construct those systems that will not only solve the immediate problems, but are sensitive to the long-term interactions that affect the sustainability of the solutions. It is only through sound development that the benefits of public health, food, energy, water, and all of society's needs and desires can be equitably distributed around the globe. Thoughtful development does not need to affect the environment adversely. Development can be long-term, efficient, effective, and ecologically beneficial.

**Design Concepts**

In accepting the challenge, I suggest a set of nine design concepts for building the foundations — the framework — for sustainable engineering.

The first design concept is education. As facilitators of sustainable development, engineers must have the skills, knowledge, and information that are the stepping-stones to a sustainable future. Before engineers can assume their facilitative role, we must remedy the deficiencies in their education. Whatever their specialty, the promotion of sustainable development demands that engineers cultivate an understanding of the environmental and economic issues, problems, and, especially risks and potential impacts of every action.

The second concept is to adopt the notion of "ecosystems" thinking. We are traditionally taught problem-solving skills that break down each problem into its simplest pieces, study each of them, and then move on to the next in a linear manner. This is almost the antithesis of synthesis, the combining of separate elements to form an integrated and whole coherent system. If we are to approach sustainable development (as we must) in a manner that imitates the natural processes around us, then engineering must become a unifying, not a partitioning discipline.

The third concept, which is related to the second, is to emphasize the aggregate consequences of what we are recommending. Practicing "ecosystems" thinking requires that engineers begin to examine more carefully the aggregate long-term consequences of decision, in terms of both time and space. We must understand the net contribution of individual impacts or decisions. This approach moves well beyond what we refer to as "environmental protection." Environmental protection in not synonymous with sustainable development.

The fourth concept is to acquire environmental economic tools to integrate the environment and social conditions into market economics. History has taught us that, for all its shortcomings and inequities, a market economy based on a free enterprise system affords the best opportunity to achieve that level of global economic development that must occur to support growing populations and sustainable development. It is not an either/or proposition, it must be both. So, within the limitations of sometimes distorted market economics, we must grapple with the need to develop and practice "environmental economics."

The fifth step is to search for sustainable alternatives. The engineer, as a project team leader or member, bears much of the responsibility for recommending the technical alternatives. However, we typically take a narrow and circumscribed approach, and we frequently fail to expand the array of requested alternatives to include those that are environmentally sustainable. We will have arrived when we would no more recommend an environmentally unsound solution than we would a *structurally* unsound solution. When we can talk to a client, or to public and private decision makers and tell them that this is not sustainable, explain why, and offer alternatives, then we will be practicing sustainable engineering.

The choices that are made determine whether the project ends up creating problems or solutions. Life-cycle consequences run along the project's entire time dimension, from planning through design, construction, operation, deactivation, demolition, and even disposal. Those consequences run spatially well beyond the project site. We must answer hard questions about disposal of materials. The true life-cycle results may extend well beyond even the life of the project — perhaps many times the life of that project.

The sixth concept is to develop and apply technology to serve sustainability. We need new technologies, from materials to processes that we haven't even dreamt of yet. Technology focused on sustainable development is a key to solving problems created in the past and preventing new ones in the future. Engineering and scientific communities must work toward the advancements in technology that will yield the basic ingredients for sustainable development.

The seventh concept is to listen to those we serve. I believe that the demand for sustainable development springs from the desires of the society we serve. We must consider sustainable development a dynamic process that responds to the continuously changing needs and an expanded knowledge base of the specific society, culture, and community we serve. Unless we can be truly relevant to societal needs, we will doom to failure even the best intentions of engineers toward achieving sustainable development. We can become so caught up in the wonders of the short-term creation of "things" that we forget the long-term and enduring effects on the people we are really serving!

The eighth concept is to cultivate a multidisciplinary team approach. And that's not new to the profession. We have been doing this for a long time, but a multidisciplinary approach in this context goes well beyond getting the electrical and the mechanical engineers together. It goes beyond the array of engineering disciplines to include many, many others. We must bring together the knowledge, skills, and insights of the physical as well as social sciences.

The ninth and last step goes back to the first — education — except in the other direction. We must continuously educate those we serve. Some of these "things" and some of the "ethics" that I am suggesting will not always appear spontaneously in the hearts of those for whom we work.

We must strive to educate all elements of society and promote universal adoption of a sustainable development ethic — particularly among private and public sector decision makers — the developers; the investors; and local, regional, national, and even international governing bodies. The engineering profession as a whole must assume a responsibility for educating not only those current decision makers, but also future engineers and future decision makers.

However these nine concepts may evolve, we, the engineers of the world, must act *now*. We must create new directions for our creative energies and technologies.

**Partnerships**

Public and private partnerships are the key. Partnerships promote innovation and efficiency. Together we can help create solutions that join economic growth with sound management of the environment and set a new direction for the world and the future.

As a nation, as a community, as a family, we suffer from the results of unsustainable decisions and trade-offs passed down from previous generations. These decisions were usually made in well-intentioned ignorance, but today our expanded awareness of the consequences of an unsustainable path provides an opportunity — no, an imperative — to change this course. Our children, and their children, deserve a future of security, stability, sustainability, and perpetual prosperity.

If we fail to accept our challenge, then the decision-making processes that influence and shape the future of our world will leave us behind. We cannot risk the consequences of a future built on an unsustainable foundation. It is up to us — the engineers and stewards of sustainable development — to see that future generations get their heritage. From my point of view, both as a soldier and as an engineer, perhaps Pope Paul VI said it best: "Another name for peace is development".

This article is reprinted with the permission of *The Bridge,* Spring 1992: 19-23.

*About the Author:*

## HENRY J. HATCH

Henry J. Hatch is the President and Chief Operating Officer of Law Companies Group, Inc., a worldwide engineering and environmental services company. A retired U.S. Army Lieutenant General, Hatch previously served as Chief of Engineers and Commander of the U.S. Army Corps of Engineers. He is a founding member of the World Engineering Partnership for Sustainable Development.

# TOWARDS UNDERSTANDING THE IDEA
# OF SUSTAINABLE DEVELOPMENT

by

## Roy F. Weston, P.E., D.E.E.

*Roy F. Weston, a well versed engineer, entrepreneur, and successful business man, has developed the following working hypothesis, definition and implementation strategies for sustainable development. The implementation strategies are adaptable to any individual, vocation or organization.*

### A Hypothesis

Planet Earth has limited and finite resources. It is the home of a marvelous, complex, ubiquitous, productive, fail-safe system of life. The life system is compose of communities of individuals in which each individual is a member of one of an hierarchy of species. Each species is interrelated to and dependent on other species supporting the community. Each fulfills a niche in sustaining life on Earth. Individuals compete with other individuals to acquire the resources needed to survive and to sustain their species.

Humans are a part of this life system. However, they constitute only about 0.002 percent of the biomass on Earth. The system is self-regulating and has sustained life on Earth for billions of years and has sustained life, as humans know it, for millions of years.

Planet Earth and its inhabitants abide by the Laws of Natural Economics. Natural economics is the science that deals with the production, distribution and consumption of the Earth's life, energy, matter, space and time resources. It consists of three, layered, interrelated, interdependent components. A physical economics component is self-regulating and abides by the Laws of Thermodynamics to control the entire system. A life system economics component is self-regulating and abides by the Laws of Biology, particularly the Laws of Ecology and Psychology to control the survivability of life on Earth. A human economics component uses human customs, institutions and laws to satisfy preferences in meeting individual "survival needs" and "aspiration exactions." Together, these components provide all the "rules of the game."

The natural economic system is driven by the decisions and actions (i.e., contributions) of individuals. Each individual has specific and universal attributes and each is constrained by the "rules of the game" and circumstances.

The life system uses radiation from the sun, as a renewable source of energy, recycled carbon and oxygen, virgin and recycled nutrients and recycled water to initiate

**40**

a food chain that supports and sustains a producer, herbivore, carnivore, scavenger and disease-producing hierarchy of life. In accordance with the "rules of the game," the non-human members of the system have, in-place, the technologies, and institutional means to meet and sustain the survival "needs" of life on Earth. The system makes contributions towards meeting human needs that are absolutely essential to human survival as well as economically beneficial towards meeting "needs" and achieving "aspirations."

Humans have reproduced, have created change (i.e., development) for their own benefit and have used the Earth's resources to implement that development. In doing so, humans have behaved naturally. Decisions and actions have been short-term, self-interest oriented. They have adopted policies and instituted practices that are creating conditions and circumstances that are neither in the short-term nor in the long-term best interests of humankind. These new and potentially harmful circumstances are growing at an accelerating rate because the human "rules of the game" are not consistent with the other "rules of the game." At this time, these human rules include neither all the technologies nor all the institutional means that are vital to communities for meeting either their current or their future "survival needs" or "aspiration exactions." That is, currently, there is extensive unsustainable development.

It is presumed that humans desire to sustain human life on Earth at a level above "survival needs." In such a case, humans must comply with the Laws of Natural Economics.

To achieve and sustain "aspiration exactions" beyond "survival needs," humans must strive to modify their attitudes and to alter their "rules of the game" towards a higher degree of self-regulation. The change would adapt the life system model to human affairs. Such adaptation requires: optimization of effectiveness and efficiency for each component of the natural economics system in order to maximize productivity, for the common good, and to minimize inefficiency and wastage; recognition that the limits and finiteness of the Earth's resources necessitates communities to attain and sustain balance among population and per member resource accessibility and requirements and capacity to meet requirements; and the application of fundamental principals to ensure a basic approach towards development.

Such a change will compel humans to recognize the roles they must fill and the accountabilities they must accept as the Earth's superior creatures. Needed change will require humans to acknowledge that they are part of the Earth's life system, that they are completely dependent on it, and that they are its natural custodian. Prudent behavior can maximize the economic benefits provided by life system products and services. Humans must strive to ensure that knowledge, prudence and reason prevail over ignorance, recklessness and greed. Humans must strive to emulate the resources conservation economics of the Earth's life system. Humans must develop sound laws, policies and practices to make them compatible with reality and supportive of the common good.

Attaining and sustaining a high standard of living and overall quality of life will depend on how well the current generation understands and adapts to the laws of the Natural Economy. With or without humankind, nature's laws will prevail. Our future and the future of our progeny depend on how well we meet the challenge of altering and enforcing our "rules of the game" so that natural behavior will enhance the common good and maximize meeting "aspiration exactions" within the reality of limited and finite resources.

# Sustainable Development: Definition and Implementation Strategies

## Definition:

Sustainable Development is a process of change in which the direction of investment, the orientation of technology, the allocation of resources, and the development and functioning of institutions meet present needs and aspirations without endangering the capacity of natural systems to absorb the effects of human activities, and without compromising the ability of future generations to meet their own needs and aspirations. (Natural resources and systems include human resources and their social systems.)[2]

## Implementation Strategies:

- Be accountable, personally; practice enlightened self-interest; and acknowledge that every individual's decisions and actions make a difference.

- Acquire and diffuse the knowledge needed to understand fundamentals and to promote informed risk taking instead of ignorant gambling.

- Protect life systems and the systems on which they depend.

- Emulate the economics of nature:

    * Maximize system efficiency and productivity in the use of energy.

    * Minimize losses and waste in the use of essential nonrenewable resources.

    * Optimize overall efficiency in the production and use of renewable resources.

- Alter humankind's cultural and institutional rules of the game to ensure the above.

---

[2] Definition is paraphrased from concept statements published as part of *Our Common Future*, World Commission on Environment and Development Report to the United Nations General Assembly, Chairperson Gro Harlem Brundtland, Oxford University Press, 1987.

Reprinted with the permission of Roy F. Weston. Adapted from his paper, " Towards Understanding, the Idea of Sustainable Development" and "Sustainable Development Implementation Guidelines for Engineers," Roy F. Weston, Inc., 1992.

*About the Author*

### ROY F. WESTON, P.E., D.E.E.

Roy Weston is the founder and Chairman Emeritus of Roy F. Weston, Inc., an international environmental and engineering services firm. His extensive 58 year career has provided him with a diverse array of environmental experience which spans the governmental, academic, industrial-petroleum, and consulting sectors. He is also a member of the World Engineering Partnership for Sustainable Development Board of Directors.

# SUSTAINABLE DEVELOPMENT — A CHALLENGE FOR THE ENGINEERING PROFESSION

by

## Don V. Roberts. P.E.

*By accident, the engineer has contributed to environmental problems. However, looking ahead, the engineer will play vital roles if the world is to achieve sustainable development. This paper summarizes the technical contributions the engineer must make in the future if global environmental problems are to be minimized. In addition, non-technical contributions are proposed to encourage engineers to emerge as environmental leaders.*

The concept of "sustainable development" was proposed by the World Commission on Environment and Development (or WCED) in 1987.

WCED was formed by the United Nations in 1984. The Prime Minister of Norway, Gro Harlem Brundtland, served as its Chairman. The Commission included 23 members for 22 countries. For three years the Commission and its staff studied the conflicts between the growing environmental problems and the desperate needs of developing nations. The conclusions of the Commission were published in the report, *Our Common Future.*

Our present situation can be summarized as follows: (Figure 1)

1. The human population has skyrocketed in the last 200 years, after thousands of years of slow growth. This sudden rise in population, along with industrialism, has produced non-sustainable demands on our global environment.

*FIGURE 1*

2. WCED concluded that it is *technically* possible to provide the minimum needs of roughly twice the present population during the next century — on a sustained basis and without continued degradation of the world's ecosystems.

3. To make the transition from unsustainable conditions to a stable or nearly stable global environment will require unprecedented global decisions and actions within the next 20 years.

Unsustainable activities today are illustrated by the following facts:

- The human population has increased by six times since the beginning of the industrial revolution (about 1790). The population has tripled since 1900. It will double again within 40-50 years.
- In this century, global economic output has increased by a factor of 20.
- The use of fossil fuels has increased by 30 times in the same period.
- Industrial production has increased by a factor of 100 times in 100 years.
- As the result of all this, 25% of the world's population in industrialized nations consumes 80% of the world's goods.
- Increased consumption has led to increased waste products, which in turn produced environmental degradation.
- For example, forests are being destroyed at the rate of 100,000 square kilometers per year. This is an area larger than The Netherlands and Switzerland combined, or an area even larger than Tasmania.
- Finally, during this century the annual loss of plant and animal species through extinction has changed from about four per *year* to more than four species per *hour*.

It is now predicted that the world's population will stabilize at about 10 billion people within the next 40 to 50 years. The world will need five to ten times the present economic development to meet the minimum needs of this larger population. This level of expanded development is considered possible by the WCED through new technologies in industry and agriculture, more effective resource management, a broader sharing of resources, and better long-term management of our environment.

The global actions required in the next 20 years assume that we can take care of the needs of a growing population using existing technology with reasonable improvements through further scientific discovery and development. However, the primary requirements will be political, not technical, in nature. Global citizens in both developed and developing nations must reach agreements on goals and objectives. Appropriate incentives and controls must be approved to achieve these objectives. Finally, effective institutions will be required at local, national, and international levels to regulate, manage and enforce the required actions.

The process illustrated in Figure 1 (page 44) is similar to an enormously complicated engineering project. We have a reasonably accurate idea of where we are at present, although many uncertainties exist. We have preliminary concepts as to the total requirements to support a larger global population on a sustained basis. The real challenge for all of us however, is to design and approve a global plan of action and to carry out this plan within the next 20 years, before it is too late.

**Role of the engineer**

Where, then, does this put us as engineers?

Frankly, I am getting tired of reading about the role that scientists will play in the future as compared to engineers. As engineers, we have poor visibility in the environmental community.

I may be biased, but I believe that the primary role of science is to help us understand and interpret the world that we live in. By contrast, I believe that the role of the engineer is more fundamental (as illustrated in Figure 2). It is the engineer who solves problems. He is faced with the need to deliver solutions within the constraints applied by time, money and available knowledge. To fill his basic role as a problem solver, the engineer must develop practical applications of available science or technology, combined with the empirical experience gained in our profession, and the ability to adapt or modify existing approaches through innovation.

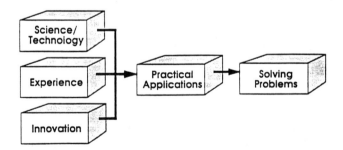

*FIGURE 2: Role of the Engineer*

In the past engineers have unintentionally contributed to global environmental problems. The population explosion resulted from reduced death rates, not increases in birth rates. Lower death rates resulted from better water supplies and sanitation, assisted by the benefits of engineer-designed hospitals and health care facilities. The growing population was fed by improved agriculture which in turn was the result of engineered land reclamation, water resource development and improved agricultural engineering. Engineers made major contributions to energy development, transportation systems and industrial production. These contributions, in turn, had a profound influence on changes in consumption patterns, the generation of industrial wastes, and the resulting environmental impacts.

I am not apologizing for the engineer. I am only trying to point out that we have contributed to global environmental problems in the past in carrying out our basic engineering roles. These same roles, applied differently in the future, could have a greater impact on achieving sustainable development than is possible through any other profession.

**Presentation approach**

In the balance of this presentation, I will develop three themes:

1. What is "sustainable development," from an engineer's viewpoint?
2. What can we do as a profession to help produce sustainable development?
3. What can we do as individuals in our daily lives to become better profession als and environmental leaders?

**Sustainable development from an engineer's viewpoint**

The World Commission on Environment and Development (WCED) de-fined sustainable development as follows: "Meeting the needs of the present without compromising the ability of future generations to meet their own needs."

To me, a sustainable system, as an engineer, is one that is either in equilibrium, operating at a steady state, or a system which changes at a rate considered to be acceptable.

The concept of sustainability is best illustrated by natural ecosystems. These function as closed "loops" that change slowly. For example, the hydro-logic or water cycle (Figure 3) involves the continuous evaporation from the ocean and other surface bodies of water up into the atmosphere. The vapor then moves over land where precipitation occurs as rain or snow. The water then returns to the ocean from surface streams or groundwater, where the process is repeated over and over.

The food cycle involving plants and animals represents another illustration. Plants grow and thrive in the presence of sunlight, moisture, and nutrients. Plants are then consumed by herbivores, and insects that, in turn, are eaten by various classes of carnivores. Resulting waste products replenish the nutrients, which allows the process to be repeated again and again.

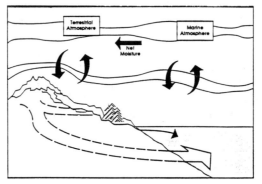

*FIGURE 3: Hydrologic Cycle*

Slow changes do occur in Nature over centuries. Climates gradually change. Some species of plants and animals evolve or ultimately disappear. In all natural ecosystems, changes usually occur at a pace that allows time for natural environmental adaptation.

By contrast, humans have used a linear approach to date. This is illustrated in Figure 4. Resources have been extracted as though they were inexhaustible. These resources have been modified or processed by industry in a manner limited only by man's ingenuity. This includes making synthetic products that have no natural counterparts.

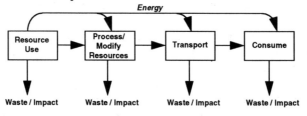

*FIGURE 4: Humans Have Used a Linear Approach to Date*

The earth's natural resources and manufactured products are then transported to the consumer. Since the 18th century, economic activity has become global in nature as the result of improved transportation systems. The volume of goods transported in international trade has increased by a factor of 800 or more. In the past 200 years, engineers have produced repeated breakthroughs in transportation systems from canals; railroads, automobiles and highways; modern shipping and port facilities; pipelines; airplanes and rockets. As consumers, we have acted as though the world has an unlimited ability to produce goods to supply our ever growing population. Finally, humans have acted as though our global surroundings can absorb any quantity of waste products.

In summary, unlike other species, we have acted as though the earth has infinite resources, an unlimited ability to produce and supply consumer products, and a limitless ability to accept our wastes. Until the beginning of the industrial revolution the energy consumed in this human once-through process and the resulting waste of resources produced only slow global changes. With a population six times as large as today, however, the linear approach used by humans cannot be allowed to continue.

**Sustainable development — the engineering challenge**

In my opinion, sustainable development will require the adoption of a human ecosystem patterned after natural processes. A proposed engineering model of such a system is illustrated in Figure 5. The use, processing, transportation and consumption of resources must flow continuously as a closed loop to the extent possible, rather than as a once-though system. Renewable resources such as fish and trees must be harvested within limits allowed by nature. The use of vital non-renewable resources, such as certain minerals, should be minimized. The manner in which we process, modify and transport resources must be conducted in harmony with the natural environment. Consumer habits must be changed with a more even distribution of goods and services.

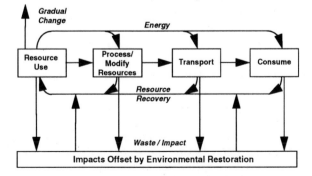

*FIGURE 5: Elements of a Sustainable System for Humans*

Throughout the process, waste must be minimized, the by-products from manufacturing and consumer use must be recycled over and over again as recovered resources. Some wastes are inevitable but should be in forms that have minimal long-term impacts on the environment. The impacts from residual waste should be offset by long-term programs to clean up and reprocess old waste sites along with other major environmental restoration programs. The energy that drives the system should be minimized by engineered improvements that promote maximum efficiency. Energy, to the extent possible, should be developed from non-fossil sources.

With a human ecosystem, some waste and loss of resources are to be expected, and long-term environmental changes are still inevitable. However, by slowing down and controlling the rate of change, it is hoped that humans and the natural environment could adapt to these changes in an acceptable manner.

The closed system shown in Figure 5 can be used to illustrate the opportunities and challenges for engineers in the years ahead.

**Resource development**

Special studies are required to inventory the world's natural resources. We need to determine which minerals will be in scarcest supply compared to projected long-term human needs. Plans must be developed to minimize the use of the scarcest resources and to create substitute materials where practical. These substitute products, however, should be biodegradable or environmentally benign. Examples include substituting composite materials for metals, optical fibers for copper, and microchips for vacuum tubes.

Improvements are needed in mining operations and mineral processing to minimize land disturbance and to reduce pollution of surface and sub-surface water. Advanced mining methods are now being developed by the US Bureau of Mines. This includes the in-situ leaching of minerals from underground ore bodies with minimal disturbance to ground surface. Other advanced mining practices include the backfilling of underground mine shafts with mine wastes during mining operations rather than allowing ground subsidence and the environmental impact of storing mine wastes above ground.

Water use must be carefully managed on a global basis. The efficiency of gravity-flow irrigation systems can be improved. (Lasers can be employed to guide machines that level growing fields, making it possible to flood them quickly and uniformly.) Trickle or drip irrigation systems can be used in arid regions to minimize evaporation and reduce the quantity of chemical salts introduced to the fields from irrigation water.

Long-term plans should be made for harvesting marine, forest and animal resources. Agricultural land must be protected from degradation. Prime agricultural properties should not be used as building sites.

**Processing and modifying resources**

Industrial wastes often contain heavy metals and synthetic organic chemicals. These materials are often toxic and are not readily degraded under natural conditions or in conventional sewage treatment plants. In the future, all manufactured products should be designed for sustainability. At a minimum they should be biodegradable. Process technology should be improved to minimize the use of raw materials and reduce the use of water and energy in industrial processing. Virtually all manufactured by-products should be suitable for reuse or recycling. The waste stream remaining should be treated at industrial sites rather than being stored or moved and allowed to escape into the surrounding environment.

**Transportation systems**

There are 500 million registered automobiles on the earth today, consuming an average of two gallons of fuel per day. This represents almost a third of the world's production of oil. If the present growth of the automobile industry continues, there will be four times as many automobiles in the year 2025 as there are today.

Future engineers will need ingenuity to create low-energy transportation systems. Automobiles should be made smaller and to operate far more efficiently. With time, individual transportation vehicles should be replaced with efficient mass transportation such as railroads and underground systems. The environmental impact of transportation options must be carefully evaluated. Improved fuels need to be developed and exhaust systems perfected. The transportation of fuels by pipelines and ships needs to incorporate improved emergency control systems and more effective remediation procedures.

**Improved consumption patterns**

Living patterns in developed nations must be modified; simultaneously, the minimum living standards must be improved in developing nations. Otherwise, our planet will never be at peace. This will require the use of less water, improved food production, more efficient transportation systems and longer-life products. Changes in food habits should be promoted. Improved systems must be developed on a global scale to process and reuse human waste.

## Resource recovery

For sustainable development to be possible, our human activities will have to be redesigned to reuse our raw materials and consumer products many times over. This will include salvaging construction materials such as concrete and asphalt from roads, the reuse of metals and other natural and synthetic materials. Extremely careful reprocessing and management of the earth's limited surface water and groundwater will be required. Waste minimization and waste reuse will have to become a way of life in both developed and developing nations.

## Environmental restoration

Since the beginning of the industrial revolution, vast quantities of harmful waste products have accumulated in abandoned waste sites. Apart from wasting resources, the chemicals from these waste sites are continuously polluting streams, groundwater and the ocean. One of the major challenges to the engineering profession will be to investigate and help clean up these sites in a cost effective manner. This also will require teamwork on the part of government agencies, industry and the public.

In the USA, abandoned waste sites are being investigated and cleaned up in an adversarial manner at extraordinary costs. The Environmental Protection Agency and other government agencies are trying to determine who generated the wastes originally. The original waste producers, in turn, are required to clean up the sites at their own expense, even if they were only partially responsible for the waste production and even if no negligence was involved at the time the wastes were originally produced. Costly site investigations are often made to avoid or establish blame rather than to develop facts sufficient for site remediation.

The public, living and working near hazardous waste sites, is justifiably worried about long-term health effects. Lawyers are profiting from litigation involving multiple parties. Delays result, and little is accomplished for the level of funds invested. In the process, engineers are exposed to enormous liability risks, without insurance.

The international approach to toxic waste site clean up should not be based on the American model. Approaches must be developed in which government, industry, and the public cooperate during waste site clean ups, in a no-fault or no-risk spirit of cooperation. The engineering profession should have incentives for innovation in solving (or even partially solving) chemical waste site problems without fear of costly lawsuits. Innovative solutions include the use of bioremediation, soil washing, in-situ flushing, vapor extraction and high temperature incineration of organic wastes.

In essence, some added environmental pollution is inevitable in the future. This must be more than offset by environmental restoration through carefully engineered projects.

**Energy production and use**

One of the greatest engineering challenges for the future will be to develop less environmentally damaging sources of energy while simultaneously reducing total energy consumption through better energy efficiency in the home, in transportation, and in industry.

Since 1850, energy use has risen 80 times — with the unacceptable production of carbon, sulfur and nitrogen as by-products. We now use more fossil fuels per year than nature produces in a million years. Fossil fuels, as a result, dump more than five billion tons of carbon into the atmosphere each year. Developing nations, such as China, will continue to rely primarily on fossil fuels for industrialization unless alternate energy sources can be adopted and justified. Even if industrial countries were to cut carbon dioxide emissions in half, the growing use of fossil fuels by developing nations will increase annual emissions of carbon dioxide to two and a half times the present level by the year 2030.

Developing new energy sources and improving existing ones represent major engineering challenges. Improved combustion processes and emissions controls are needed. Nuclear power may see a rebirth, assuming engineering problems surrounding safe nuclear energy generation can be solved, and assuming acceptable nuclear waste repositories are constructed. Additionally, engineered improvements are needed to develop practical solar and geothermal generation, wind power and biomass generation. Hydroelectric power should be developed where the environmental changes can be accepted.

Perhaps the greatest opportunity for engineers is to develop ways to reduce energy use in resource extraction, manufacturing, transportation, and in the home and work place. There is widespread agreement that improvements in energy efficiency can be made more economically than developing new supplies of energy.

Several forms of energy conservation represent important engineering challenges:

1. Energy efficient construction in homes and the work place through the use of better insulation, more efficient lamps and better use of sunlight.
2. Greater use of co-generation — combined production of heat and electricity in industry. Only one-third of the steam energy in a conven-tional power plant is converted to electricity; much of the remaining steam energy can be used for heating and other industrial purposes.
3. Better furnaces in industry. China and India use four times as much energy to make a ton of steel as Japan does. US steel plants could reduce their energy use by 40%.
4. Smaller, more efficient automobiles. Better yet, greater use of mass transportation systems using electricity from non-fossil sources.

**What can the individual engineer do?**

The preceding paragraphs summarize a few of the ambitious challenges to our entire engineering profession. But what can we as individuals do that will make a difference? I believe this falls into four categories:

1. Become informed about environmental issues.
2. Inform others.
3. Do a better job of environmental planning on your projects.
4. Become environmental leaders and decision makers.

**Become informed**

In the past 100 years, engineers have had to cope with an explosive growth of technical information. This forced us to specialize in fields such as civil, mechanical, chemical and electrical engineering. Within individual fields such as civil engineering, multiple sub-fields have evolved such as structural, sanitary, geotechnical, and highway engineering. In our formal training as engineers, less and less time is devoted to history, economics, and literature. We get little training in writing skills and public speaking. Of even greater concern, most of us have little formal exposure to environmental sciences such as geology, hydrology, meteorology, chemistry, biology and agronomy.

I believe that each of us has an obligation to become better informed about the world in which we live and the social, economic and environmental problems we face in the future. In the past two years, I have read perhaps 100 environmental books and papers. This has been a stimulating and broadening experience for me personally. I encourage each of you to broaden your reading and talk to professionals in other disciplines. Become involved in multi-disciplined projects. Each of us should try to become better environmental generalists while maintaining our specialized field of practice.

**Inform others**

As you become better informed about the earth around you and develop broader project experience, I urge each of you to share this information with others. Give presentations. Talk about environmental issues with your friends. Give talks at professional meetings and at public gatherings. Participate in public hearings and legislative procedures. Attend meetings with ardent environmentalists; many of them need exposure to economics and technical reality.

In the future, I believe the engineering profession should become far more involved with the transfer of engineering experience. The practical knowledge that we learn on projects will need to be shared with Eastern Europe and between developed and developing nations throughout the world.

Two suggestions for technology transfer come to mind:

1. Create a worldwide "senior mentor program," and
2. Create "regional development centers" to assist developing nations.

As we approach retirement years, many of us should volunteer to help developing countries — as advisors to environmental agencies and as mentors to local engineering firms. Perhaps a "senior mentor program" could be established by international engineering organizations such as the International Federation of Consulting Engineers (FIDIC) with the assistance of national engineering societies and the World Bank. This program would coordinate the voluntary assistance by late-career professionals including engineers, planners, economists, ecologists and other environmental specialists. This plan might by considered the late-career equivalent of the voluntary "Peace Corps" in America with the exception that highly skilled professionals would be involved in economic development, environmental protection, and restoration.

With the rapid improvement in global communications systems, engineering throughout the world may soon be interconnected through electronic communications systems. This network would open the way to part-time senior mentor activities by experts willing to volunteer a few hours of each week without having to leave a computer keyboard at home or the office. The value of such voluntary part-time help might be increased by storing environmental experience in special computer programs called "expert systems." (Such systems allow the use of artificial intelligence to summarize knowledge obtained from experts regarding procedures, strategies, rules of thumb, etc. in special problem areas.)

The concept of senior mentors might be expanded to include the creation of "regional development centers." These regional centers could coordinate teams of consulting environmental engineers, international lenders, local university personnel and other volunteers. These centers could be used as a substitution for sending students from developing nations to European or American universities. Programs would be tailored to the specific needs of developing countries, including the use of technology that would be appropriate locally. Centers could be used for long-term regional development planning, baseline environmental studies, independent review of controversial projects and post-construction monitoring. Regional centers might also be used to provide training to young environmental engineering students from industrialized countries.

### Better environmental planning on projects

I believe each engineer should try to improve the way environmental issues are considered in project planning. Many of the current procedures to conduct environmental impact analyses (EIAs) were developed in America in the 1960s. By accident, the process became flawed or different than intended.

In my opinion, environmental impact studies as they are performed today, are often wasteful and ineffective. Typically environmental studies are performed in the sequence illustrated on Figure 6.

A project is proposed, with as specific site in mind. Biological and other environmental studies may be delayed until after a project has been evaluated and feasibility studies started or completed. By this time, the project may have already drawn attention and opposition from environmentalists and government agencies. The environmental studies may become a battleground between those who wish the project to go ahead and those who wish to have it

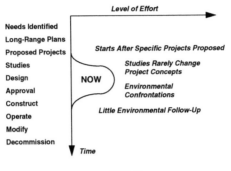

FIGURE 6

stopped. Both advocates and opponents may perform independent studies of the environment, generating massive amounts of data. The environmental studies may have little real influence on the outcome of the design. Wasteful environmental studies may result, and significant legal costs can follow. Environmental confrontations may result in lengthy delays.

Assuming the project is finally approved, there may be little monitoring of construction or the environmental consequences of the completed project. As a result the actual impacts of the project may be different from that predicted during the original studies.

Some planners are now considering a better approach to environmental studies on projects, such as illustrated in Figure 7. This involves starting sooner and continuing longer in environmental planning. Strategic plans are needed for the economic development of many countries. These long-range strategies

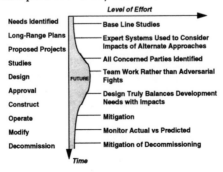

FIGURE 7

should strike a reasonable balance between the needs for development (to meet the needs of a growing population) and the needs for environmental protection. Baseline studies of the regional environment should be made years before actual projects are proposed. I believe that the results of such environmental baseline studies could be summarized globally in computerized expert systems and GIS Data. Expert systems might be used to predict environmental impacts, if only crudely, as part of long-range developmental studies.

After it is concluded that some form of economic development is required to meet the needs of a region or country, efforts should be made in the planning process to identify all parties who may have a legitimate reason to be concerned about balancing developmental needs with environmental protection. To the extent possible, planning of environmental studies should include direct input from all concerned parties. Better approaches need to be developed including public involvement to promote cooperation from the very beginning rather than wasting energy, time and money through confrontations and adversarial relationships.

Once planning has started on a project, environmental studies should gradually increase in scope as the project alternatives are defined. Environmental constraints, if any, can be considered completely when all of the project options are developed. The environmental studies should include long-term environmental economic costs of the project — including indirect costs resulting from off-site environmental pollution. Cultural and sociological issues should also be considered. Environmental monitoring should be continued during and after construction. Provisions should be made to modify the design, if necessary, when the environmental impact is different than predicted. Environmental monitoring should continue throughout the life of the project, even through the decommissioning of the facility.

**Engineers as environmental leaders and decision makers**

To date, engineers have had little visibility as environmental leaders. Political bodies in my country are dominated by lawyers, with very few individuals possessing a technical or engineering background. Engineers are rarely seen in political circles. The reasons may include the following:

- Most engineers have technical training that is narrow and highly specialized.
- Many engineers may be too theoretical to deal easily with social, political or economic problems.

- Engineers may be politically naive.
- Engineers are often poor communicators. Many dislike interacting with the public.

It is my belief that engineers have two choices to make in the future. They can remain as technical advisors to government agencies and clients or emerge as environmental leaders and decision makers. It is too late for most of us to make the choice as individuals. However, I think it would be possible to make a difference within one or two generations.

The profession could evolve to provide political leadership by the sequence illustrated in Figure 8. Perhaps one-fourth of engineers of the future should be recruited to become superb environmental generalists. This might be done by widely publicizing the real contributions that engineers make in analyzing and solving environmental problems. Children should be recruited to become environmental/political/engineering leaders as early as age 12. Scholarships could be offered to gifted children, providing a broad education which combines the technical skills of engineering with a wide range of environmental disciplines. These studies would be integrated with a background in economics, law, history, and literature, as well as the political sciences. Special leadership training would be mandatory, especially in developing communication skills.

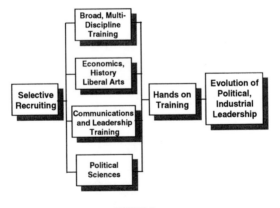

FIGURE 8

A variety of early assignments could give the students practical exposure. One possibility would be to create the equivalent of an "Environmental Engineering Youth Corps" that would provide hands-on experience under the guidance of mentors, assisting government agencies in the design and construction of projects in developing nations. Through collaboration with consulting engi-neers, industry and government agencies, the "integrated environmental engineers" might be prepared to enter industrial and governmental leadership roles by the time they are in their mid-20s. With time, the new environmental engineers might even displace attorneys for leadership in political processes.

**Putting it all together**

In summary, as engineers we are living at a time of dramatic challenges. Global environmental problems are rapidly approaching a crisis; we helped create this crisis. Solving these global problems will require enormous changes of both a political and technical nature. Our challenges are summarized in Figure 9. They are:

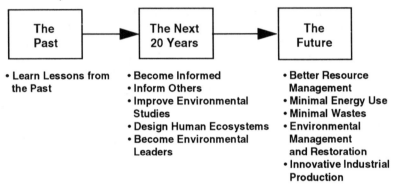

| The Past | The Next 20 Years | The Future |
|---|---|---|
| • Learn Lessons from the Past | • Become Informed<br>• Inform Others<br>• Improve Environmental Studies<br>• Design Human Ecosystems<br>• Become Environmental Leaders | • Better Resource Management<br>• Minimal Energy Use<br>• Minimal Wastes<br>• Environmental Management and Restoration<br>• Innovative Industrial Production |

*FIGURE 9: Putting It All Together*

1. We need to understand and learn from the past.

2. In the next 20 years, we must:

   • Become informed
   • Inform others
   • Improve the ways we conduct environmental studies
   • Design our projects as closed loop ecosystems to the extent possible
   • Become environmental leaders.

3. In the long run, engineers have the opportunity to lead the way in:

   • Better resource management
   • Innovative industrial processes
   • Modified transportation systems

- Minimal energy use
- Minimal waste
- Better environmental management and restoration.

Our challenge as a profession is unmatched. If we wish, we can continue to fill purely technical roles. However, our potential value in achieving sustainable development will not be realized unless we become environmental leaders and effective decision makers.

This article is reprinted with the permission of the author, Don V. Roberts, and *Transactions,* a publication of the Institution of Professional Engineers-New Zealand, (Phone: 64-4-473-9444).

*About the Author:*

## DON V. ROBERTS

Don Roberts is the President of the World Engineering Partnership for Sustainable Development (WEPSD). He serves as Vice President and former Director of Corporate Planning and Development for CH2M Hill, an international environmental engineering and design services firm. Roberts, a founding member of the WEPSD, holds more than 40 years experience in environmental and geotechnical engineering, He is responsible for major studies on 500 environmental engineering projects located in 20 countries.

# Engineering to Sustain the Environment

## by

## DAVID THOM

*"We travel together as passengers on a little spaceship, dependent on its valuable reserves of air and soil; all committed for our safety to its security and peace; preserved from annihilation only by the care, the work, and I say the love we give our fragile craft".* - Ambassador Adlai E Stevenson to the 39th session of the United Nations Economic and Social Council, July 9, 1965.

To attain the goal of sustainable use of our planet's resources it is now recognized that all those concerned with the development, selection, and use of technology have a heavy responsibility. Technology is now seen as the key link between humans and nature. The engineering profession must now accept the challenge to lead the way. It is a time when the whole future of technology is the subject of much thinking worldwide.

Some of this thinking, it is pleasing to relate, has been done by others - the diplomats, lawyers, scientists, agriculturists, foresters, planners, manufacturers, business people and citizens who have worked in various capacities and forums in the two year process of preparatory meetings and negotiations that provided the working documents for the 1992 United Nations Conference on Environment and Development (UNCED).

The two lots of thinking reach similar conclusions about the role of engineering as society struggles towards sustainable development - the alternative to catastrophe. The role is distinctively different from the comfortable niche in which, buoyed by the astounding success of technology, we have been settled for at least 50, and maybe, 100 years. The good news is that, at last, the issues are emerging with the stark clarity of the New Zealand Alps on a clear morning. The bad news is that this stark clarity points to challenge and change, travail and trauma, and the dangers and discomforts of leadership.

In this address, I will trace the development of these ideas through to the invention of the concept of sustainability. At that point, we will pick up the two separate strands of thinking, the engineers on the one hand, and the general public, as represented by the UNCED and its background effort, on the other. Then we will see how these strands can be merged into one set of conclusions about the strategic future plan for engineering, and the role that, if we have the stomach and determination to pursue, will achieve an eminence and respect for engineering that it has not formerly enjoyed, even at the height of the Victorian period.

It is just 30 years since the early 1960's. At the beginning of that decade no one was worried about the environment. Humankind was to be carried by technology into a golden age. By the end of that decade there had been an awakening. Rachel Carson published *Silent Spring*.[3] A number of significant conferences had been held. In the USA the outcome was the National Environment Protection Act, a benchmark piece of legislation - not only for the USA - but world-wide, because it invented the Environmental Impact Statement as a device to compel the examination of environmental consequences on the one hand, and the consideration of these effects by decision makers on the other.

In the two decades of the 70's and 80's, (just 20 years mind you), one can follow another two streams of development, this time divergent streams. There is first the evolution of environmental institution and capacity building at the international and national level. At the international level were the United Nations Conferences on the Environment (1972), Habitat (1974), and Population (1976). From the 1972, Stockholm Conference came the United Nations Environment Programme, the Earth Watch monitoring system, a global fund, and other initiatives. At the national level, in an uneven pattern determined by relatives of problems, cultures, finances and state of development, we see laws being passed, government institutions like departments for the environment being established, and procedures put in place like EIA (the process) and EIS, a statutory reporting step in the process.

The second and comparative pathway has comprised the bad news. Again, bear in mind I am talking about a 20 year period. World population in 1970 was 3.7 billion. In 1990, it was 5 billion, up 35 %. In 1980, the handling and disposal of hazardous wastes was recognized as a national and global issue. The forests and lakes of Europe and North America were affected by acid rain. In 1985, came confirmation of a prediction made in 1974. The ozone shield over the Antarctic was thinning and a hole had developed. There followed unprecedented international action culminating in the Montreal Protocol of 1987 and the Helsinki Declaration of 1989 stating the intention of 80 countries to phase out CFC's by the year 2000. Another greater and more complex global problem was growing. By the 1980's, concerns about increasing $CO_2$ levels, expressed by a few scientists in the 1960's became shared by a large proportion of the scientific community. Data showed increasing concentrations, not only of $CO_2$, but also of nitrous oxide ($NO_2$), methane ($CH_4$) and specific fluorocarbons. There are, currently, various forecasts for global warming and climate change, and consequential rises of sea level. Elsewhere, there was famine, and pollution, deserts were expanding, fish stocks were declining and the destruction of tropical forests was accelerating.

If one looks at the two divergent paths, then, the race was being lost. Whatever was being done in the way of institution and capacity building, environmental deterioration was taking place at a much faster rate. Enter the World Commission on Environment and Development from an urgent call by the General Assembly of the United Nations. After three years of travel, study, and hearings, the Commission in 1987 published its now famous report, *Our Common Future (1987)*. The fundamental theme is relationships, systems, and interdependence. Everyone should read it, but here are some major points:

- There are no separate crises of environment, development and energy. They  are all part of one crisis.

- We borrow environmental capital from future generations with no intention or prospect of repaying.

- Governments have failed to make the bodies whose policy actions degrade the environment responsible for ensuring that their policies prevent that degradation.

- The ecological dimensions of policy must be considered at the same time as the economic, trade, energy, agricultural and other dimensions.

- Governments should develop long term, multi-faceted population policies and campaigns to pursue broad demographic goals.

- Loss of species and threats to ecosystems have become a major ecnomic and environmental hazard.

- The planetary system would not stand the raising of developing world energy use to levels comparable with the developed world.

- Between 1985 and 2000, cities would grow by another three quarters of a billion people.

- A new world economic order is required in which (i) the sustainability of ecosystems on which the global economy is required must be guaranteed, and (ii) economic partners must be satisfied that the basis of exchange is equitable.

- The Law of the Sea Treaty must be ratified as soon as possible.

- Without institutional change, and new laws that anticipate the pace and scale of environmental problems, the goals of *Our Common Future* would be unattainable.

*Our Common Future* was the precursor to the UNCED 1992, and it is almost time to discuss the thinking about the role of engineering that went on in that five year period, and the outcomes of the immense amount of work that provided the basic documentation to the UNCED. Before that, however, let us cement into place two of the building blocks for the remainder of the address - sustainability, and ecosystems.

If *Our Common Future* can be encapsulated in one word, (which it can't), that word is 'sustainability'. This report defines sustainability as "meeting the needs of the present without compromising the ability of future generations to meet their own needs". We all know, in a general sort of way, what this means but philosophers of a "how many angels can sit on the point of a pin" variety have been inclined to insist that it must be more precisely defined before we can go further. The New Zealand Resource Management Act, the stated purpose of which is 'to provide the sustainable management of natural and physical resources' has a more detailed definition (p.21).

*Sustainable management* is defined as 'managing the use, development, and protection of natural and physical resources in a way, or a rate, which enables people and communities to provide for their social, economic, and cultural well-being and for their health and safety, while:

(a) Sustaining the potential of natural and physical resources (excluding minerals) tomeet the reasonably foreseeable needs of future generations; and

(b) Safeguarding the life-supporting capacity of air, water, soil and ecosystems; and

(c) Avoiding, remedying, or mitigating any adverse effects of activities on the environment.

Ralf Buckley in *"Policy Tools for Sustainable Development"*, a paper to the 1992 Conference of Institutions of Engineering-Australia's Committee on Engineering and Environment suggests that an activity is ecologically unsustainable if it causes impact which would (i) probably interfere with ecosystem processes or components; and (ii) probably be irreversible, for technical or social reasons.

*'Interfere with ecosystem processes....?'* There is the bottom line — of Buckley, the New Zealand Resource Management Act, *Our Common Future*, and the World Conservation Strategy. "An economy that is developing sustainability adapts and improves in knowledge, organization, technical efficiency and wisdom, and it does this without consuming, co-opting, or divesting, beyond some point, an ever greater percentage of the matter and energy of the ecosystem, stopping at a scale at which the ecosystem can continue to function and renew itself year after year. Such an economy is therefore one in which the life of the ecosystem, its services, and consequently, the economy, can be maintained for a long time."

Some people have drawn an analogy with capital and interest. We live in a world of degraded and degrading ecosystems, but these are the productive and reproductive capital of the planet. Sunlight is the driving force and photosynthesis is the process. The plants and the animals and the gene pools are the stock. This is all that all life, including humans, has to work with.

The processes of nature are cyclic, and to illustrate this point I wish to turn the work of Don V. Roberts, a consulting engineer from Colorado whose study of the role of engineering has been a major contribution to the ideas put before you today. Don Roberts considers that natural ecosystems function as closed 'loops' that change slowly. The hydrological cycle, for example, involves continuous evaporation from the oceans and other surface bodies of water. Vapor moves over land. Precipitation occurs as rain or snow and returns to the ocean via rivers, streams, and groundwater. The process cycles endlessly. Water is essential to the food cycle on which all animal life is dependent. Plants grow and thrive in the presence of sunlight, moisture and nutrients. Plants are consumed by herbivores which in turn are eaten by various classes of carnivores. Waste products replenish the nutrients and the process cycles on.

By contrast, humans have used a linear approach. Resources have been extracted as though they were inexhaustible. These resources have been modified or processed by industry in a manner limited only by man's ingenuity. This includes making synthetic products that have no natural counterparts.

The earth's natural resources and manufactured products are then transported to the consumer. Since the 18th century, economic activity has become global, and the volume of goods transported on international trade has increased by a factor of 800 or more. In the past 200 years, engineers have produced repeated breakthroughs in transportation systems from canals, railroads, automobiles and highways, modern shipping and port facilities, pipelines, aircraft and rockets. As consumers, we have acted as though the world has an unlimited ability to produce goods and services to supply our ever-growing population. Unlike other species, we have acted as though the earth has infinite resources, an unlimited ability to produce and supply consumer products, and a limitless ability to accept our wastes. All this can be described as a linear, not cyclic, approach, and the advent of acid rain (now affecting northwestern Japan), the ozone hole, pollution, climate change, all indicate how profoundly technology is involved.

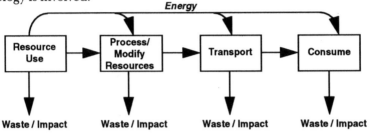

FIGURE 1

In contrast, sustainable development will require the adoption of a human ecosystem patterned after natural ecology systems.

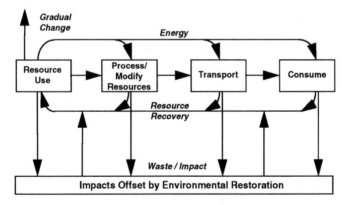

FIGURE 2

The use, processing, transportation and consumption of resources must flow continuously as a closed loop to the extent possible, rather than as a once through system. Renewable resources such as fish and trees must be harvested within limits allowed by nature. The use of vital non-renewable resources should be minimized. The manner in which we process, modify and transport resources must be conducted in harmony with the natural environment. Throughout the process, waste must be minimized; the by-products from manufacturing and consumer use must be recycled over and over again as recovered resources. Some wastes are inevitable but should be in forms that have minimal long term impacts on the environment. The impacts from residual waste should be offset by long term programmes to cleanup and reprocess old waste sites along with other major environmental restoration programmes. The energy that drives the system should be minimized by engineered improvements that promote maximum efficiency. Energy, to the extent possible, should be developed from non-fossil sources.

This diagram indicates the immense scope of the challenge now presented to the engineering profession.

In using Don Roberts' thoughts and diagrams, I have introduced you to some of the engineering thinking of the past five years. Here it is important to point out that institutional development is vital in order to introduce the dynamics that promote change. In the case of the engineering profession, institutional development has been provided by the World Federation of Engineering Organizations (WFEO) Environment Committee, founded in 1979, some environment committees within national engineering societies, and the task committee on environment set up by the International Federation of Consulting Engineers (FIDIC) in 1989. By 1987, the WFEO Committee had produced its code of environmental ethics, sometimes described as visionary, inspirational, and unenforceable. This is hardly the terminology of enthusiastic endorsement, but as time goes on the code looks less visionary and more realistic - which says a lot for the vision.

In 1991, the WFEO Environment Committee recommended to the General Assembly of WFEO a statement on the future role of engineering that had been prepared by the joint efforts of the environment committees of the Institutions of Engineers of Australia and New Zealand. This statement was adopted by WFEO and referred on to the UNCED Secretariat, then engaged in the final stages of preparing documentation for the UNCED.

In parallel with these developments, FIDIC's Task Committee had been studying the role of consulting engineers in preventing or minimizing environmental problems. Studies were arranged (Don Roberts' investigation was one of these) and papers and workshops introduced into the programmes of the annual meetings of the Federation in Oslo (1990) and Tokyo (1991). The outcome was the FIDIC policy statement.

So much for the thinking of the engineers - for the time being. Now, let me turn to the outputs from that massive two year process of preparation and preparatory committees and negotiation and protocols that reached its culmination in the UNCED Conference, Rio De Janeiro, June 1992.

Many of those who saw in the UNCED a last chance to face the global problems of environmental management, and who believed that timetables and binding commitments were essential, were deeply disappointed by these outcomes. Others have seen the conference as a success because it brought the global community together in an unprecedented way and because the tangible results each represent an agreed pathway on which future commitments can be established.

What were these outputs?

1. The Rio Declaration on Environment and Development;

2. 'Agenda 21', the pathway to sustainable development in the 21st Century;

3. A statement on Forest Management Principles;

4. The UN Framework Convention on Biological Diversity, opened for signature, and signed by 153 countries at the conference;

5. The UN Framework Convention on Climate Change, opened for signature, and signed by 153 countries at the conference.

The Rio Declaration represents a set of 27 agreed principles aimed at the objective of 'a new and equitable global partnership', 'international agreements that respect the interests of all and protect the integrity of the global environment and developmental system', and recognition of 'the integral and interdependent nature of Earth, our home'. Some of the principles are summarized below:

• Humans are entitled to a healthy and productive life in harmony with nature.

• The environmental and developmental needs of future generations should be heeded.

- All states and people shall cooperate-operate to reduce poverty.

- The situation and needs of developing countries shall be given special priority.

- States shall cooperate-operate in global partnership to conserve, protect and restore the health and integrity of the Earth's ecosystem.

- States should reduce and eliminate unsustainable patterns of production and consumption and promote appropriate demographic policies.

- States shall cooperate-operate to strengthen endogenous capacity builing.

- Environmental issues are best handled with the participation of all concerned citizens.

- States should enact effective environmental legislation.

- The precautionary approach shall be widely applied.

- National authorities should promote the internalization of environmental costs. The polluter should bear the cost of pollution.

- Environmental impact assessment shall be used for activities likely to have an adverse effect on the environment.

- States shall immediately notify other States of natural disasters likely to produce sudden harmful effects.

- Indigenous people have a vital role in environmental management and development.

- Warfare is inherently destructive of sustainable development. Peace, development and environmental protection are interdependent and indivisible.

The outcomes of the discussion of 'Agenda 21' occupy more than 450 pages. 'Agenda 21' is the operational plan for moving humankind into the age of sustainability. It should be read and given profound consideration by all people, including all engineers. Its implementation will demand the commitment and the capacity of all nations, peoples, and individuals.

More than half the sections of 'Agenda 21' are of direct or indirect relevance to science and technology (e.g. those dealing with the protection of human health, human settlement, integration of environment and development in decision making, protection of the atmosphere, integrated approaches to the planning and management of land resources, combating desertification and drought, sustainable mountain development, conservation of biological diversity, environmentally sound management of biotechnology, toxic chemicals, hazardous wastes, solid wastes, radioactive wastes, scientific and technological community, transfer of environmentally sound technology, education, national mechanisms, institutional arrangements, and information.)

Chapter 8 of the Rio 'Outcomes' addresses integrating *environment and development in decision making,* a fundamental theme of environmental management. It notes that "An adjustment or even a fundamental reshaping of decision making, in the light of country-specific conditions, may be necessary if environment and development is to be put at the center of economic and political decision making, in effect achieving full integration of these factors". Chapter 8 recommends national review of policies to ensure the progressive integration of environmental and developmental issues, and the strengthening of institutional structures. It also recommends the systematic monitoring and evaluation of development processes and the state of the environment, and the development of national strategies for sustainable development. 'Laws and regulations suited to country-specific conditions are among the most important instruments for transforming environment and development policies into action', says chapter 8, which goes on to recommend the establishment of a cooperative-operative training network for sustainable development law, and the development of effective national programmes for review and enforcing compliance.

**The Statement on Forest Management Principles**

The non-legally binding statement of principles for a global consensus on the management, conservation and sustainable development of all types of forests is immensely significant as it is the *first* global consensus on forests.

**Convention on Biological Diversity**

The role of biological diversity in environmental management has been already mentioned, together with the dangers of the extraordinary and accelerating rate of loss of species. This is occurring, ironically, at a time when biotechnology is likely to greatly increase the range of chemical and medicinal benefits to be gained from plants. Loss of species can increase the risk of instability in ecosystems, a risk that may be increased further by ozone, acid rain, and climate-change. Under the Biodiversity Convention, contracting States are responsible for:

- Conservation and sustainable use of biological diversity;

- Developing national strategies and plans;

- Integrating conservation and use of biodiversity into national strategies and plans;

- Identifying processes likely to have significant adverse effects;

- Maintaining identification and monitoring activities;

- Establishing a system of protected areas;

- Adopting incentives for conservation and sustainable use of components of biodiversity;

- Establishing education and training programmes;

- Promoting and encouraging research;

- Requiring environmental impact assessment of programmes and policies likely to have adverse impacts on biodiversity;

- Assist access to genetic resources by other contracting parties.

**Framework Convention on Climate Change**

The ultimate objective of this convention is to achieve stabilization of greenhouse gas concentrations in the atmosphere at a level that would prevent dangerous anthropogenic interference with the climate system in a time frame sufficient to allow ecosystems to adapt naturally to climate change. (This refers to the possibility that ecosystems may become over- stressed and fail beyond some unknown rate of change.)

The *Convention on Climate Change* states a number of principles including:
1.   The climate system will be protected for the benefit of present and future generations on the basis of equity. Developed countries will take the lead.

2.   Specific needs and special circumstances of developing countries should be given full consideration.

3.   The precautionary principle shall apply.

4.   Parties have a right to and should promote a supportive and open international economic system.

Contracting parties to the *Convention on Climate Change* enter into the following commitments:

(a)   To develop, update, and publish national inventories of emissions and removals by sinks.

(b)   To formulate national and regional programmes of measures to mitigate climate change.

Both the Biodiversity Convention and the Climate Change Convention incorporate institutional mechanisms for implementation through a permanent conference of the parties, to be convened for its first year within one year of the convention coming into force. A similar mechanism is established for the non-binding statement of Forest Principles. A UN Commission is to be created to examine progress with the implementation of 'Agenda 21'.

Implementation of 'Agenda 21' will require major legal and institutional action at national levels. Every section of 'Agenda 21' deals with objectives, basis for action, and means of implementation. These include a review of legal systems, the setting up of new institutions, financing, and education.

'Agenda 21' and the two conventions also have immense implications for engineering. *Our Common Future* talked of "the re-orientation of technology, the key link between humans and nature". With UNCED, the programme for this re-orientation was put in place.

## RIO OUTCOMES - Some Implications For Engineering

### The Rio Declaration

All engineering .... should study and reinterpret the Rio Declaration into engineering related guidelines.

### Agenda 21

The precautionary principle should be understood and applied.

All engineers should be fluent in environmental impact assessment and use it as a tool for selection of technical options.

Develop education and training programmes that enhance the capacity of the engineering profession to contribute to 'Agenda 21' outcomes.

Foster the transfer of technical information, particularly for the assistance of developing countries.

Develop the understanding of, and the facility and techniques for the integration of technology into the social, environmental, and cultural context.

### The Convention on Biodiversity

Note that conservation of the productive capacity of ecosystems, is fundamental to sustainable development, and review all engineering practices in this light.

Ensure that all engineers receive general education about ecosystems, earth systems, and the Convention on Biodiversity.

Contribute to development and monitoring of national strategies, plans and programmes for conservation and sustainable use of Biodiversity.

### The Convention on Climate Change

Promote research in and implementation of energy efficient policies, technologies, and practices.

Promote research in and implementation of technologies that eliminate or reduce emissions of greenhouse gases, particularly in relation to energy, transportation, industry, and waste disposal.

Promote research into and application of sustainable energy technologies; e.g. hydro, solar, wind and tidal sources of energy.

Participate in and contribute to the development and monitoring of national policies related to climate change.

Foster the transfer of information about mitigating technology, especially to developing countries.

Consider and allow for the risks of rising sea level in relation to low lying areas, and the need for additional warning and protection against storm events.

**A Global Strategic Plan for Engineering**

It should be stressed that in summarizing the thinking done with WFEO and FIDIC and in bringing forward a few pointers from UNCED outcomes, we are reporting the outputs of a process, not the ideas of one individual. UNCED outcomes are the output from a huge process - in effect the global strategic plan. The outputs from the Engineering Committee, Task Groups, and the General Assembly are totally consistent with and complementary to UNCED Outcomes. Of these, more than half the sections of Agenda 21 and the two conventions, are of direct or indirect relevance to science and technology. We can glimpse the strategic plan for engineering that lies within the global strategic plan of 'Agenda 21'. It is a plan that addresses and bears out a prescient forecast made in *Our Common Future* in 1987.

*"The fulfillment of all these tasks will require the reorientation of technology-the key link between humans and nature'" - Our Common Future.*

It's not that what we learn of engineering science will be different - but the whole ethos of practice will be different. Engineers would aim and train to be constructive and very positive contributors to policy development. The fundamental basis of practice would be protection, and, where necessary, restoration of natural systems. This would require a serious review of ethical responsibilities, an education that would produce a facility to think through technological options and impacts in a parallel way, the ability to work with facility and creativity in multi-disciplinary groups, and a strong social interest.

Engineers are familiar with the question of lead time - we are dealing with it often on our projects. We should give some thought now to lead time in relation to the challenge now facing the future of our profession. Already, we have clearly seen that global institution building has not kept pace with the developing crisis. Through this period we have, as a profession, and if we are honest with ourselves, lagged rather than led. Rate of change is, however, still increasing. World population increase is now running at one billion per decade. By 2010, world population will be 7000 million, up 40 per cent from the 1990 level. One fifth of the world's population is now starving. One billion people are consuming three quarter's of the world's resources and creating much of the pollution that is threatening irreversible damage to ecosystems. Perhaps a quarter of the earth's total biological diversity, about one million species, is in serious risk of extinction over the next 20 to 30 years.

Lead time is now, therefore, a serious issue both at the global level, and at the level of the profession whose business and duty is the reorientation of technology. The message is that we don't have all day - we no longer have the luxury of setting our own pace and deciding our own responses when pushed to do so by a growing public opinion. 'Agenda 21' has set out the global strategic plan. We, the great proponents of lead times, systematic planning, and deliberate action must attend to some global business in which our future is vitally concerned. What shall we do, when shall we do it by, and how?

In the technical area, we are lagging further behind racing events. Let me give some examples:

(i) I have been to Paris recently to attend a Ministerial Meeting and Senior Level Seminar about 'Cleaner Production'. This focused on the management, the technologies, the data-bases, and the policies that underpin and drive the concept of manufacturing that uses resources with great efficiency and eliminates off-site treatment of wastes.

(ii) Some countries in Europe are considering legislation that will require return of products to manufacturers after use. Such requirements would force a new dimension into the design of products. Some major car manufacturers are already looking at this approach. Engineers in Europe are thinking already about buildings of which materials and components are designed to be recycled into the next generation of buildings.

(iii) The concept of Life Cycle Analysis, the analysis of a product for efficiency of resource use, efficiency of energy use, and performance in every relevant environmental criteria from the 'cradle to the grave' is being applied in laboratories and universities in Europe. Such analysis will become the basis of product labeling on the shelves of retail and supermarket outlets. It will also become the basis of purchase by a public that is already demonstrating a willingness to pay more for products that have an environmental guarantee.

(iv) A present phenomena is the development of data-bases that have world-wide access like the EPA/UNEP International Cleaner Production Information Clearinghouse (ICPIC) and UNIDO's Industrial and Technological Information Bank INTIB, and another UNIDO data-base, CLEANTECH DATA.

(v) Regional centers on 'Cleaner Technology' are being sponsored by UNEP, and UNESCO has produced guidelines for the establishment of University Chairs in 'Engineering and Environment.'

Let us continue with education and ask what approach to engineering education do we need **now** - not in five years. It will take five years to create a significant shift in the basic philosophy of engineering education, another five to produce the first 'new age' engineers, and five more before they are starting to exert influence. Fifteen years from 1992 is 2007, so the lead time is too great to start with. But there is not time to debate that question. All engineers must be environmentally competent as professionals, that is they must be knowledgeable and well read in the field, they must have command of technologies, and they must be accepted into or rejected from their professional body on that basis. In short, a public that will within five years be totally environmentally conscious, must be able to put complete trust in the technologists. What is meant by techniques? For the civil engineer, this means total command of environmental assessment as a tool and the ability to use it to creatively fashion products onto which an environment/sustainability label can be put. The analogy lies with Life Cycle Analysis and Cleaner Production, the equivalent tools of the chemical, mechanical, electrical and manufacturing engineers. There's much more to be said here, too, but there is only time for one more, fundamental comment. The agents of the technological re-orientation - of the key link between humans and nature - must have a better understanding of the fundamentals than what they have now. There must be something about the basics of global systems and the principles of ecosystems in the basic education, and understanding of every engineer.

We can see this if I expand briefly on the ethical question. It is beyond question that use of technology has had an enormous impact on what is called 'life support'. Let me mention ozone, climate change, acid rain, and biodiversity. Doctors swear an oath with respect to their responsibility for life. How different now is the position of the technologies? We must confront and decide this question, because our future is bound up in the answer.

In this summary of 'Agenda 21' engineering (or engineering for the 'New Industrial Revolution') is overlaid on Don Robert's diagram, which looks like this.

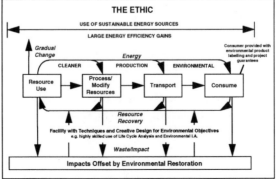

THE ETHIC

USE OF SUSTAINABLE ENERGY SOURCES

LARGE ENERGY EFFICIENCY GAINS

*Gradual Change*

*Energy*

Consumer provided with environmental product labelling and project guarantees

CLEANER       PRODUCTION       ENVIRONMENTAL

| Resource Use | → | Process/ Modify Resources | → | Transport | → | Consume |

*Resource Recovery*

Facility with Techniques and Creative Design for Environmental Objectives
e.g. highly skilled use of Life Cycle Analysis and Environmental I.A.

*Waste/Impact*

Impacts Offset by Environmental Restoration

*GREATLY IMPROVED UNDERSTANDING OF NATURAL SYSTEMS / ECOSYSTEMS*

How shall we do it? Institutional development is essential to coping with change. The WFEO and its Environmental Committee are institutional agents that can assist with change, as are environmental committees at the regional and national level. Professional bodies that have established environment committees have been able to make substantial progress.

In March of 1992, engineers and other environmental leaders came together in New York and agreed to develop the concept of a World Engineering Partnership for Sustainable Development. The concept is now being elaborated. The means of delivery was seen as regional centers, related perhaps to WFEO's regional structure. A regional center would function as a data center and clearing house, and a source of information on all aspects of sustainable development. It would be the focus of an environmental engineering and sustainable development center network that links together the national engineering institutions of the region. It would be available to provide support to the governments of the region in facilitating access to information on appropriate technology and appropriate environmental and sustainable development standards, and in providing support to environmental agencies involved in environmental management, technology assessment, and environmental assessment. It would have the role of encouragement of capacity building in each country in regard to environmental engineering education. It would work to provide international exchanges of personnel, and the establishment of international teams to examine trans-national regional issues.

Effort is under way to secure funding for a feasibility study for a center in our Federation of Engineering Institutions of South East Asia and Pacific (FEISEAP) region. Last November, the FEISEAP executive meeting in Hong Kong agreed to support the project and a detailed programme to enlist additional support is in process.

To conclude: All the indicators - ozone, climate change, loss of biodiversity, population, acid rain - show that the contest between technology and nature has now reached an advanced and dangerous stage. If it remains a contest, nature will win, but it does not have to remain a contest. We, the technologists, faced with the challenge of reorienting technology, have a choice between two paths. We can trail behind the accelerating pace of events until the widening gap leads to a rejection on the basis that we are no longer relevant. Or, we can use our formidable abilities in the setting of objectives and the methodical realization of goals, accept challenge, change, trauma and travail and march in the vein of the new Industrial Revolution.

**78**

One thing we must always remember, engineering is a human construct, a convenient subdivision of human activity that allows a focus on an objective, a subdivision whose boundaries are drawn up for our convenience. Nothing is acknowledged of such things in the cyclic systems of nature, endlessly looping, cycling, feeding back and oscillating. And it is the relationship between technology and nature, and the role of our profession must now play in that relationship, that is the fundamental theme of this address. In nature, in the words of the poet, "If I pick a flower, I disturb a star."

---

[3]Carson, Rachel. *Silent Spring.* Houghton Mifflin, 1962.

Reprinted with permission of the author. First presented to The Society of Professional Engineers of Papua New Guinea Conference, Lae, Papua New Guinea, November 1992.

*About the Author:*

## DAVID THOM

David Thom is a professional engineer from New Zealand. He is Chairman of the WFEO Committee on Engineering and Environment and a major contributor to the engineering for sustainability movement. Among his many other activities, he is currently working to establish a regional engineering center in the FEISEAP region. He is a member of the World Engineering Partnership for Sustainable Development Board of Directors.

# Sustainable Development References:
# An Annotated Bibliography

The following references will provide the reader with additional sources of information on sustainable development, sustainable technology, and the environment.

# Sustainable Development References

**Backs to the Future: U.S. Government Policy Toward Environmentally Critical Technology** . George R. Heaton Jr. *et al.*, Washington D.C.: World Resources Institute, June 1992. *

Criticizes science and technology policies of the Bush Administration and provides an extensive list of environmentally critical technologies that can bring about large and cost-effective reduction in environmental risk. These include new devices for energy capture and storage, agricultural biotechnology, alternative agricultural, new manufacturing systems, separation technologies, precision fabrication, etc. Such new technology is central to a sustainable economy, and the only viable basis for long-term growth and competitiveness.

**Beyond Compliance: A New Industry View of the Environment.** Edited by Bruce Smart (Senior Fellow, World Resources Institute; former US Undersecretary of Commerce and CEO of Continental Group). Washington D.C.: World Resources Institute, April 1992. 285p. $19.95pb. *

Societies worldwide are pursuing two potentially conflicting goals: a cleaner environment and sustained economic growth. Reconciling these goals will require a sweeping technological transformation - essentially an "eco-industrial revolution." Provides case studies of some two dozen companies that have publicly stated a determination to move toward environmental excellence: the Pollution Prevention Pays program at 3M since 1975, the Recycled Paper Coalition involving three large San Francisco Bay Area companies, the comprehensive environmental program of Pacific Gas & Electric Co, the Weyerhaeuser intensive forest management strategy, Dow Chemical's Responsible Care initiative, the Business Charter for Sustainable Development sponsored by the International Chamber of Commerce (signed by over 500 companies from 35

**Note:** * The majority of these annotated references were contributed by or adapted from *The Future Survey,* Michael Marien, ed., a publication of The World Future Society, 7900 Woodmont Avenue, Suite 450, Bethesda, MD 290814. (301) 656-8274. The World Future Society, an association for the study of alternative futures, is a non-profit educational and scientific organization founded in 1966. The Society acts as an impartial clearinghouse for a variety of different views and does not take positions on what will happen — or ought to happen — in the future.

countries as of 12/31/91), the Monsanto Pledge, innovation by Briggs Nursery in raising its ornamental nursery stock (an example of a small company improving the environment), cooperation between Allied Signal Inc. and Tufts University in forming The Environmental Literacy Institute at Tufts (for training faculty members and integrating environmental issues into all undergraduate, graduate, and professional school curricula), Du Pont's Environmental Leadership Council, and the Royal Dutch/Shell Group's use of scenarios in planning.

**Changing Course: A Global Business Perspective on Development and the Environment.** Stephan Schmidheiny (Chairman, BCSD; World Trade Center, Geneva; and Chairman, UNOTEC). Cambridge MA: MIT Press, May 1992. 374p. $35.00;16.95pb. *

Schmidheiny, a Swiss industrialist who heads three major holding companies, was asked by Maurice Strong to serve as principal advisor to UNCED for business and industry. This led to forming the Business Council for Sustainable Development; among the 50 members are the heads of ALCOA, Browning-Ferris, Chevron, ConAgra, Dow Chemical, Du Pont, Mitsubishi, Nippon Steel, Nissan Motor, Northern Telecom, Royal Dutch/Shell, and Volkswagen. The BCSD has already organized some 50 conferences, symposia, and issue workshops in over 20 countries. A 3 page Declaration of the BCSD states that business will play a vital role in the future health of the planet, that economic growth and environmental protection are inextricably linked, that "economic growth in all parts of the world is essential "to sustain growing populations", and that new forms of cooperation between government, business, and society are required. The world is moving toward deregulation and private initiatives. This requires corporations to assume more social, economic, and environmental responsibility. "Progress toward sustainable development makes good business sense because it can create competitive advantages and new opportunities."

Chapters discuss "alarming trends" in patterns of development and in environmental degradation, meeting the challenge of "eco-efficiency" by profound changes in the goals and assumptions that drive corporate activities, redefining the rules of the economic game to move from wasteful consumption and pollution to conservation, "full-cost pricing" that includes environmental costs, altering standard national accounts and GNP calculations, making energy markets work by market signals that move toward sustainability, increased energy efficiency, financing sustainable development in emerging capital markets, free trade and sustainable development, managing corporate change with the vision of sustainable development, the innovation process in pollution prevention and materials substitution, Multinational corporations as primary agents of technology transfer, sustainable agriculture and forestry, and Less Developed Country leadership for sustainability. Half of the book is devoted to 38 case studies on making energy conservation pay, the CEO as Chief Environmental Officer, environmental auditing, long-term partnerships, catalyzing improved supplier performance, cooperating with stakeholders, and managing cleaner production and products. [**NOTE:** Cutting-edge thinking for business.]

**Choosing a Sustainable Future.** Report of the National Commission on the Environment (Russell E. Train, Chair). Washington D.C.: Island Press, Jan. 1993 180p. $25.00; $15.00pb. *

The 19-member Commission convened by the World Wildlife Fund (including Peter A. Berle, Alice M. Rivlin, Madeleine Kunin, and James Gustave Speth) recommends sustainable development as a primary goal of environmental and economic policy, implementation of Agenda 21, promoting technology compatible with sustainable development, taxing environmentally harmful activities, revising measures of economic activity, fostering an environmentally literate citizenry, shifting away from fossil fuels as quickly as possible, and environmentally-sensitive management of public and private land. If leadership is based on a new ethic of environmentally responsible behaviors; it is far more likely that the coming years will bring a higher quality of life. (**NOTE:** Few of these proposals are new; what is important is their integration into a broad agenda and endorsement by a mainstream, group.)

**Coming Clean.** Ken Beecham *et al.*, London; *DTTI/* (Distributed the by International Institute for Sustainable Development-Winnipeg), May 1993. 64p. C$25.00 (204-958-7700). *

The first international survey of corporate environmental reporting analyzes over 70 companies in Europe, North America and Japan that have produced free standing environmental reports. There is a growing number of companies who are producing these reports, following such bellwethers as Monsanto and NorskHydro. They are doing so because of growing pressure to report on the sustainability of their products and processes, their success in taking advantage of opportunities related to sustainable development, the growing recognition that business must move beyond mere compliance, and support of "corporate citizenship" codes of conduct that promote best environmental practice.

**Corporate Environmentalism.** (Focus Issue). *Columbia Journal of World Business* (310 Uris Hall, Columbia University), 27:3-4, Fall-Winter 1992, 297p.

The 30 essays are under six headings: 1) **Sustainable Development:** Frances Cairncross on the growth of mass environmental consciousness, Stephan Schmidheiny on the Business Council for Sustainable Development, a politics of hope (connecting a clean and safe environment with a healthy economy); 2) **Markets:** market innovation as a powerful tool of environmental policy (tradable permits, debt-for-nature swaps, the proper allocation of property rights), the modification of capital markets to incorporate environmental costs and benefits and promote long-term investment; 3) **Treaty-Making:** the new global negotiations at UNCED, new corporate roles in environmental treaty-making, trade and environmental protection, the corporation as an NGO in international policy-making; 4) **Regional Policies:** Japan's "New Earth 21" policy for sustainable development, environmental policy in the EC, the European Environmental Agency and its "Toward Sustainability" program of year 2000 objectives, the 1991 German Packaging Order to reduce and recycle packaging waste, shifting the US tax burden to unproductive activities of resource waste and pollution (by Robert Repetto of WRI), implementing the Montreal Protocol to restore the ozone layer, environmental technology cooperation between transnational corporations and LDCs; 5) **Energy and Technology:** S. Fred Singer on the detrimental effects of a carbon tax, the inevitability of increasing carbon emissions, energy management in Eastern Europe and the former USSR, the need for revolutionary restructuring of philosophic and technologic underpinnings; 6) **Corporations:** the role of the private sector in environmentally friendly development, getting a strategic edge on environmental innovation, lessons from companies recognized as environmental leaders (the environmental vision must be tied to specific goals carefully tailored to the organization), the increasing accountability of companies to the environmental expectations of stakeholders, corporate environmental communications, steps toward "sustainable communication," environmental option assessment (a new tool to support decision-making as regards substance life cycle management). [**NOTE:** Leading-edge thinking, handsomely produced.]

**Costing the Earth: The Challenge for Governments, The Opportunities for Business.** Frances Cairncross (Environment Editor, *The Economist*). Boston MA: Harvard Business School Press, March 1992. c300p. $24.95. *

Public interest in green issues may ebb and flow, but politicians and business managers will find some environmental pressure irresistible and lasting. "Environmental issues will not go away." However, bad government policies may make even more of a mess than the unfettered market. A better starting point is to look for ways to improve markets, (e.g. clear rights of ownership for natural resources and making sure that consumers and producers pay the true costs of the environmental damage they cause). Setting a rough environmental value may be a better basis for policy than none at all. Economic growth cannot be made environmentally benign, "but greener growth is possible". Chapters explain the environmental limits to sustainable growth, discount rates, measuring costs and benefits, anti-environmental farm subsidies, making polluters pay, conserving energy, international environmental management, the challenge to companies (the demand for cleaner products and processes will change the way they think about innovation), green consumerism (the ultimate oxymoron for the most ardent environmentalists), waste disposal, recycling, and effective corporate environmental policy (a clear statement of principles and objectives, regular environmental audits, harnessing the enthusiasm of employees, building environmental considerations into accounting procedures, creating links with local people). Concludes that "a truly green company in unlikely to be badly managed. Conversely, a well-managed company finds it relatively easy to be green." [ALSO SEE: **Leading Your Business in the Environmental Age** by Steven J. Bennett and Richard Freierman (Wiley, July 1992.320p.$24.95).]

**Design for the Environment.** Dorothy Mackenzie, New York: Rizzoli International Publications, 1991. 176p. $35.00 h.b.

This beautifully illustrated book provides guidance on the challenge of "designing green". An environmental approach in the whole design-to-production cycle means decisions must be made about choice of materials, minimization of resources; type of energy source; industrial treatments; the length of life for products and how to recycle or otherwise dispose of waste products. With numerous illustrations and case studies from practicing designers in the UK, US, Europe, and Japan, this book delves into how enormous improvements can be made in the use of materials without sacrificing aesthetics or function.

**Dictionary of Environment and Development: People, Places, Ideas, and Organizations.** Andy Crump, Cambridge, MA: MIT Press, April 1993. 272p. $16.95pb.

This concise reference offers a guide to a host of new terms that are being spawned as environment and development issues move to the forefront of international concerns. Booklet covers ecological processes such as desertification, tropical diseases, financial and agricultural terms, international treaty organizations and acronyms, and much more. Handy desktop reference.

**The E-Factor: The Bottom-Line Approach to Environmentally Responsible Business.** Joel Makower (Editor, *The Green Business Letter*, Washington). New York: Times Books/Tilden Press, March 1993. 292p. $23.00. *

Being "green" boils down to two essential goals: reducing waste and maximizing resource efficiency. The E-Factor is a part of doing business, incorporating environmental thinking in positive and profitable ways throughout a company. Chapters are devoted to six key concepts: 1) **Economics:** the new understanding of relationships between economics and ecology (ecological economics, life-cycle analysis, emissions trading); 2) **Enforcement:** growing pressures on companies to improve their environmental performance (and consequences from failure to do so); 3) **Empowerment:** the importance of leadership and corporate vision in fostering change; 4) **Education:** the need for communication, openness, and new partnerships between companies and their customers, suppliers, regulators, stockholders, and the general public; 5) **Efficiency:** the need to integrate the ideas of pollution prevention, waste reduction, energy efficiency, and process redesign; 6) **Excellence:** the need to merge Total Quality Management principles with environmental practices. Concludes with some essentials to keep in mind: Don't try to be perfectly green (you can't), start with a project likely to be a success, get top-level approval, involve everyone, challenge suppliers and competitors to meet or beat your goals, and give proper recognition and rewards. As companies put the E-Factor into operation, employees will be likely to express these same ideals in their private lives.

**Earth in the Balance: Ecology and the Human Spirit.** Senator Al Gore, Jr. (D-Tenn). Boston: Houghton Mifflin, January 1992. 402p. $22.95. *

Our ecological system is crumpling as it suffers a powerful collision with a civilization out of control. "We must make the rescue of the environment the central organizing principle for civilization." This means embarking on an all-out effort to use every policy and program to preserve our ecological system. A "Global Marshall Plan" is proposed, with five strategic goals: 1.) world population stabilization, 2.) environmentally appropriate technologies developed through a global Strategic Environment Initiatives, 3.) a new global "economics" that redefines GNP and productivity, 4.) a new generation of treaties and agreements, and **5.**) a cooperative plan for educating the world's citizens. [**NOTE:** Remarkable, sophisticated, and well-informed thinking by a world-class political leader for the 21st century. ALSO SEE: **World on Fire: Saving an Endangered Earth** by Senate Majority Leader George J. Mitchell of Maine (Scribner's, Jan 1991), which has similar ideas, but no focus on technology and education; and **Global Environmental Politics** by Gareth Porter and Janet Welsh Brown (Westview, Dec 1991. 208p. $43.50; $10.95pb).]

**The Earth Summit's Agenda for Change: A Plain Language Version of Agenda 21 and the Other Rio Agreements.** Michael Keating. Geneva, Switzerland: Centre for Our Common Future (52, rue des Paquis), April 1993. 70p. $10.00pb (20 or more copies, $7.50 each). (Also available in French, German, Italian, Russian, and Spanish). *

A brief and popularized version of AGENDA 21, along with shortened versions of 1) the Rio Declaration on Environment and Development (stating that environmental protection should be an integral part of the development process, etc), 2) the Statement of Principles on Forests (committing nations to take part in "the greening of the world," etc 3) the UN Framework Convention on Climate Change (requiring nations to provide information on greenhouse gases they release and how much is absorbed by their sinks, etc), and 4) the Convention on Biological Diversity (requiring nations to develop national strategies for sustainable use of biodiversity, restore degraded ecosystems, etc). Following the Preamble, AGENDA 21 is condensed here into four sections: **1) Social and Economic Dimensions:** international cooperation, combating poverty, changing consumption, controlling population, protecting and promoting health, sustaining human settlements, making decisions for sustainable development; **2) Conservation/Management of Resource:** protecting the atmosphere, managing land, deforestation, desertification and drought, mountain development, rural development, biodiversity, managing the oceans and fresh water, safer use of toxic chemicals; **3) Strengthening the Role of Major Groups:** to include, women, children and youth, indigenous people, NGOs, local authorities, farmers, workers and trade unions, business and industry, scientists; **4) Means of Implementation:** financing sustainable development, technology transfer, science, education and public awareness, creating capacity, organizing for sustainable development, international law, and information for decision-making. [**NOTE:** This 70-page version has a different arrangement than the 321-page "abridgment" (above). Both extend a widely-shared guiding vision for many people worldwide.]

**Ecological Economics.** Edited by Robert Constanza. New York: Columbia University Press, Sept. 1991. 525p. $50.00. *

Derived from the first biannual conference of the International Society for Ecological Economics, held in 1990. In contrast to conventional economics, EE takes a wider view and longer view of systems, and sees the human economy as part of a larger whole. The macro goal of Ecological Economics is sustainability of the combined ecological/economic system. Some policy recommendations: promote long term thinking and use of a systems approach, institute a consistent goal of sustainability in all institutions at all levels, ease up on income taxes and implement fees on destructive use of natural capital, and develop transdisciplinary curricula for our over specialized education system.

**Ecology, Economics, Ethics: The Broken Circle.** Edited by F. Herbert Bormann and Stephan R. Kellert (both Professors, School of Forestry and Environmental Studies, Yale University). New Haven CT: Yale University Press, Dec 1991. 233p. $26.50.

Essays from a 1989 lecture series at Yale: Edward O. Wilson on the need to appreciate and preserve biodiversity, Norman Myers on biodiversity and global security, David Ehrenfeld on the management of diversity as a paradox (it often reduces diversity), Wes Jackson on nature as a measure for sustainable agriculture, David Pimental on the costs and benefits of pesticide use, Holmes Rolston III on environmental ethics as duties to the natural world, Paul H. Connett on waste strategies in the disposable society, William Goldfarb on the abuse of groundwater, Gene E. Likens on who is responsible for toxic winds, Malcolm Gillis on the role of resource accounting in mending the broken circle for tropical forests, William A. Butler on incentives for conservation, and Thomas Eisner's proposal for a substantial increase in "chemical prospecting" (the exploratory process by which new and useful natural products are discovered).

The editors view ecology, economics, and ethics as parts of a whole, but with weak linkage. They also view a "global environmental deficit" which, like its economic counterpart, also borrows from the future. But it differs from trade and budget deficits in that its implications are far greater and not easily reversed. Neither economics nor ecology can provide a sufficient basis for coping with the current environmental crisis. To mend the broken circle, fundamental alterations are needed in how we perceive the natural world and how we act in an ethically responsible fashion. Such a shift in ethical consciousness cannot be achieved unless humans develop a far greater sense of humility, respect, and even awe toward nature.

**Empowering Technology.** Edited by Lewis M. Branscomb, Cambridge, MA: MIT Press, August 1993. 304p. $17.95 pb.

Experts from Harvard's Center for Science and International Affairs examine a key set of issues and problems that, taken together, define the scope and limits of technology policy and its role as a strategy for redirecting the American economy. Among the topics discussed are the new relationships between federal and state governments implied by the Clinton administration's proposals, the usefulness of the concepts of "critical technologies" for setting priorities, the creation of new missions for the national laboratories, the changing nature of the social contract between the government and research universities, the problems that will confront the creation of a national information infrastructure, and the relationship between education and the requirements for work in the twenty-first century.

**Environmental Problems and Sustainable Futures: Major Literature from WCED to UNCED.** Michael Marien (Editor, *Future Survey*), *Futures,* 24:8, Oct 1992, 731-757. (Also published in *UNESCO Future Scan,* #2.) *

A bibliographic essay on environmental literature reported in *Future Survey* (FS) during the five years bounded by the 1987 report of the World Commission on Environment and Development and the 1992 UNCED Earth Summit. Attention is focused on a framework for assembling the literature, based on two major categories: 1) **Environmental Problems**: to include, global overviews (planet earth in peril, regions and nations, human population growth), global climate change, endangered resources (overviews, biodiversity, deforestation, land and protected areas, freshwater, wetlands, oceans), pollution (air and water, other), waste and hazards (solid and toxic waste, nuclear waste and radiation, natural hazards); 2) **Toward a Sustainable Future**: to include, new environmental thinking (ecophilosophy), elements of a sustainable society (general overviews and agendas, ecological agriculture, green technology and transportation, energy, cities and communities, other sectors), actors and environmental movements, government, and information frontiers. In all, 312 items are cited in 255 footnotes, each with *FS* or **FS Annual** reference numbers. An appendix lists 81 English-language periodicals relevant to environmental movements, government, and information frontiers. The 68 strictly environmental titles are listed by date of first publication; the median date is 1982, suggesting a doubling in the past 10 years. Concludes that green infoglut is a neglected problem.

**Environmental Strategies Handbook: A Guide to Effective Policies and Practices.** Edited by Rao V. Kolluru, New York: McGraw-Hill, Inc., 1994 1030p $79.50hb.

Featuring contributions from more than 30 experts from the associated fields of environmental science, public health, business, and law, this handbook offers insights into how industries can develop optimal environmental strategies and integrate them into long-term strategic plans to ensure growth and competitive advantage at the national and international levels. The book also features a listing of regulatory agencies, industry associations, and environmental consulting firms and support groups that can assist executives in profitably linking corporate ambitions with environmental stewardship and sustainable development. An excellent, thought provoking reference!

**Getting at the Source: Strategies for Reducing Municipal Solid Waste.** World Wildlife Fund. Washington D.C.: Island Press, June 1992. 142p (8x11"). $15.00pb.

Final report of the WWF Strategies for Source Reduction Steering Committee, which addresses the question of "How can the design and use of products be altered to reduce the amount and toxicity of municipal solid waste?" Proposals include: 1) a national definition for source reduction that suggests multiple actors and multiple activities; 2) wide adoption of a three-part Life-Cycle Assessment model consisting of: an inventory of materials, energy used, and environmental releases at all stages in the life of a product or process; an analysis of potential environmental effects; an analysis of needed changes; 3) setting a national policy goal that serves to inspire — rather than dictate — implementation plans by others and quantifiable goals for specific sectors of the economy; 4) a framework for evaluating source reduction opportunities; 5) an annual national awards program for outstanding achievement in municipal solid waste source reduction (recipients could include manufacturers, public interest groups, state and local governments, and educational institutions); 6) programs for labeling consumer products as "environmentally preferred" and "standard setting"; 7) various types of research (developing methods to measure the amount of waste generated and the extent of source reduction accomplished, improving social/psychological knowledge of waste generation patterns); 8) various strategies that can be implemented now (backyard composting, charging households by the quantity of garbage, using non-toxic paper and inks).

**Global Change and the Human Prospect: Issues in Population, Science, Technology, and Equity.** Sigma Xi, The Scientific Research Society, Research Triangle Park, NC.: Forum Proceedings, November 1991. 294p. $18.50pb.

This book provides impressive insights into a 1991 Sigma Xi forum attended by more than 650 participants from the fields of academia, business, industry, and government and includes such high caliber thinkers as Tom Malone, Peter Raven, John Gibbons, George Brown, Jr. and others. The proceedings call for new institutional arrangements to realize the potential of an *attractive* human prospect that an expanding knowledge base has brought within reach. Rather then delving into the symptoms of global change, such as ozone depletion pollution, etc., the attendees focused on the driving forces behind these and related problems in order to address their root causes. The book makes a strong case that it is timely for the community of natural, social, and engineering sciences to address these matters.

**Human Development Report 1993.** United Nations Development Programme, Oxford University Press, May 1993. 230 p. $29.95; $17.95 pb. *

The fourth annual volume in a groundbreaking series, asserting that "people's participation is becoming the central issue of our time" and proposing five pillars of a people centered world order. These include: 1.) new concepts of human security that stress the security of people, not only of nations; 2.) new models of sustainable human development that promote investing in human potential and creating an enabling environment; 3.) new partnerships between the state and market to combine market efficiency with social compassion; 4.) new patterns of national and global governance to accommodate the rise of people's aspirations and the steady decline of the nation state (decentralization of power can be one of the best ways of empowering people); 5.) new forms of international cooperation that focus directly on the needs of people rather than on the preferences of nation states. As in earlier Reports, HDR 1993 discusses trends in human development and supplies 92 pages of human development indicators, including a composite Human Development Index. (**NOTE:** Original, sophisticated, important.)

**The International Politics of the Environment: Actors, Interests, and Institutions.** Edited by Andrew Hurrell (Nuffield College, Oxford) and Benedict Kingsbury (Exeter College, Oxford), Oxford & NY: Clarendon Press (Oxford UP), July 1992. 49p. $79.00; $19.95pb. *

Not only has the number and scope of transborder environmental problems increased; a new category of *global* environmental issues has emerged. These problems affect everyone, and can only be effectively managed by cooperation of all or virtually all states. Chapters discuss the adequacy of international environmental law (a new concept of "responsible" sovereignty is emerging), international environmental regimes, negotiating more effective international agreements, NGOs and the legal protection of the oceans, problems of negotiating a treaty on climate change (by Elliot L. Richardson), the role of the UN system, the role of the World Bank, the EC and international environmental policy (the EC has already adopted 280 items of environmental legislation, and is exerting pressure on the US), the costs and benefits of an alternative course of action against global warming (by economist Wilfred Becherman, who argues that there is "plenty of time" to think about this), US policy toward the global environmental policies, allocating costs between rich and poor nations, Amazonian deforestation, and the proposed Global Forests Convention leading to a World Forests Organization and a Tropical Forests Fund (by Norman Myers).

**The Island Press Bibliography of Environmental Literature.** The Yale School of Forestry and Environmental Studies (Joseph A. Miller *et al.*). Washington D.C.: Island Press, January 1993. 396p. $48.00. *

The 3,084 briefly annotated books (published through 1991) and journals are arranged in two parts of seven sections each. Within each section, items are subdivided into groups of 10 to 40 references. **Natural Environment:** 1) whole earth systems and conditions (global resources, ecology, etc.); 2) air and atmosphere; 3) water and hydrosphere; 4) land; 5) plants and agriculture; 6) forests and forestry; 7) animals. **Human Environment:** 8) society and culture (country studies, population, movements); 9) ethics and arts (philosophy, religion, nature writing and thought); 10) law and government; 11) economy and business; 12) health and medicine; 13) engineering and technology (solid waste, recycling, hazardous waste, water engineering); 14) science and research (information sources, reference books, journals, modeling, statistics). Includes an author/title index, a subject index, and a Quick-Reference index of general topics. [**NOTE:** Treats each item equally, with no indication of outstanding works.]

**Nature, Technology, and Society: Cultural Roots of the Current Environmental Crisis.** Victor Ferkiss (Professor Emeritus of Government, Georgetown University). New York: New York University Press, March 1993. 341p. $40.00. *

Author of **Technological Man** (1969) and **The Future of Technological Civilization** (which proposed "ecological humanism" in 1974) discusses early views of nature and technology (the Greeks, Romans, Jews, and Early Christians), how technology flourished during the renaissance (a movement toward a scientific-technological conquest of nature), the industrial revolution and the beginnings of technocracy, views of nature and technology (in America, in Marxist socialism, in Islam, and in the Orient), technological cornucopianism (Arthur C. Clarke, Herman Kahn, R. Buckminister Fuller, Gerard O'Neill), contemporary critics of technology (Jacques Ellul, Murray Bookchin, Garrett Hardin, Lewis Mumford), ecofeminism and ecotheology, deep ecology thinking (Arne Naess, Gary Snyder, Ernest Callenback), and the global green movement. Concludes that the drive to conquer nature through technology is virtually universal, although the modern Western world has been the leader. But technology is not irresistible, and human cultures can choose which to resist. New, less-polluting technologies can be encouraged or discouraged by government policies. We must also radically reevaluate what our self-interest really is. The world needs a spiritual revolution - a basic change in values, and a new concept of progress. We must end the male (or at least "macho") quest to dominate nature, and rethink our place in nature.

**Our Common Future.** World Commission on Environment and Development (G. H. Brundtland, Chair). Oxford University Press, June 1987. 383 p. $9.95 pb. *

This independent commission, chaired by Gro Harlem Brundtland (Prime Minster of Norway) with Mansour Khalid of Sudan as vice chair, was established by the UN General Assembly in late 1983, due to widespread frustration in the international community about the ability to address vital global issues. It was intended as a sequel to the Brandt Commission's **Common Crisis** (MIT Press, 1983) and the Palme Commission's **Common Security** (Simon and Schuster, 1982). Members of the WCED came from 21 nations, and public hearings were held on five continents. The report defines "(Sustainable development) is development that meets the needs of the present without compromising the ability of future generations to meet their own needs." A sweeping report which includes recommendations regarding: 1.) Population; 2.) Food Security; 3.) Species and Ecosystems; 4.) Energy; 5.) Industry; 6. )Urbanization; 7.) Managing the Commons; 8.) Peace and Security; and 9.) Institutional and Legal Change. This publication is a "must read" for those interested in sustainable development and some of its intellectual underpinnings.

**A Post-Rio Compact.** James Gustave Speth (Former President, World Resources Institute, Director, United Nations Development Programme), *Foreign Policy,* #88, Fall 1992, 145-161. *

With the end of the Cold War, the goal of diplomacy is shifting from conflict management to common endeavor. The UNCED Earth Summit suggested that the new axis of world affairs is not East-West, but North-South. America's policy toward developing countries has been in disarray for years, and is due for reinvention. The US should declare a new international mission committing itself to a new era of concerted international action against poverty and environmental deterioration. The Foreign Assistance Act should be totally rewritten. Seven elements of a new US program that reflects the needs of the developing world and America's long-term interests: 1) the prime objective must be to promote sustainable development through effective family planning, sustainable agriculture and forestry, sustainable energy production, and effective pollution control; 2) traditional development assistance must be extended to such critical areas as access to capital and technology; 3) the US should concentrate on building human and institutional capacities needed for sustainable development; 4) overall financial support for development assistance should be increased, perhaps doubled; 5) the US program should directly address global environmental threats that affect all countries; 6) efforts to promote wise investments must be coupled with internal reforms such as unwise subsidies and waste of water and energy; 7) the new US program should promote multilateral approaches where possible. To carry out these objectives, a new Global Policy Council should replace the National Security Council, and the Agency for International Development (AID) should be replaced by a Sustainable Development Cooperation Agency (SDCA). The SDCA would include a Sustainable Development Foundation to make grants and an Institute for Scientific and Technical Cooperation.

**Recycling Solid Waste: The First Choice for Private and Public Sector Management.** Thomas E. Duston (Associate Professor of Economics, Keene State College, NH). Westport CT: Quorum Books/Greenwood Press, April 1993. 204p. $55.00. *

"Recycling has come of age: it can be the first choice for solid waste management in the vast majority of waste disposal situations in the U.S." It can also be the first choice (the least costly method) for the more specialized solid waste where people live, work, and play: office buildings, shopping malls, warehouses, schools, colleges, and recreation areas. Chapters discuss the anatomy of a solid waste system, stages of a well-planned recycling program, the microeconomics of recycling, and integrated waste management. Appendices include New Hampshire guidelines for composting yard waste, vendor lists of various recycling technologies, a sample recycling brochure, etc. [**NOTE:** Duston served as chairman of the committee that initiated a recycling program in Chesterfield NH, reducing the town solid waste budget by 35%.]

**Shaping Cities: The Environmental and Human Dimensions.** Marcia D. Lowe, Worldwatch Paper #105, Washington D.C.: Oct 1991. *

Good planning is essential to cities. Various ideas are described to free cities from auto-centered problems, enhance energy efficiency, protect water supplies, promote a variety of affordable housing, devote more space to trees, promote urban agriculture, arrest destructive sprawl, and achieve "compact growth".

**State of the World 1993: A Worldwatch Institute Report on Progress Toward a Sustainable Society.** Lester R. Brown *et al.*, New York: W.W. Norton, January 1993. 268p. $19.95; $10.95pb. *

The 10th annual assessment, now printed in 27 languages, warns of continuing environmental deterioration partly due to an economic accounting system that misleads and a biological accounting system that hardly exists. Worldwatch President Lester Brown notes intensifying global interest in the planet's future and countless examples of local gains; nevertheless "the broad indicators show a continuing wholesale deterioration in the earth's physical condition." Other chapters address widespread signs of water scarcity and how to move to water security, reviving coral reefs, closing the gender gap in development, supporting indigenous peoples, providing energy in developing countries, rediscovering the benefits of rail transportation, preparing for peace instead of war, reconciling trade and the environment, and the new industrial revolution toward sustainable practices that could be furthered by a "green industrial" strategy. (**NOTE:** As always, fresh focus on key ideas, notably green taxes.)

**Technology and Environment.** Edited by Jesse H. Ausubel and Hedy E. Sladovich, Washington, D.C.: National Academy Press, 1989 .221p.

This book is one of a series of publications designed to bring national attention to issues of the greatest importance in engineering and technology by the National Academy of Engineering. The book considers the proximate causes of environmental damage - machines, factories, cities, etc. - in a larger societal context, from which the will to devise and implement solutions must arise. It helps explain the depth and difficulty of such issues as global warming and hazardous wastes but also demonstrates the potential of technological innovation for constructive impact on the planet. With a range of data and examples, the authors cover such topics as "industrial metabolism" of production and consumption; the environmental consequences of the information era; and the design of environmentally compatible technologies.

**Toward A Sustainable World.** *ReVision: A Journal of Consciousness and Transformation,* 14:2, Fall 1991, 55-110. (Single copy $7.00 from Heldref Publications, 1319 18th St NW, Washington DC 20036.) *

Essays largely from a March 1991 conference on "Comprehensive Strategies for Sustainability" sponsored by the Harvard Center for Psychological Studies in the Nuclear Age. Topics include Donella H. Meadows on systems thinking and restructuring systems, Roger Walsh on a psychology of sustainability (on the importance of acknowledging our fundamental ignorance), Charlene Spretnak on ecofeminism and our Eurocentric acculturation that cuts off males from nature and the mother/female, Duane Elgin on a positive vision of a sustainable future and an ecoterrain way of life ("we need to discover the story that symbolizes the next stage in our evolutionary agenda and that acts as a catalyst for our energy and enthusiasm"), Stephen Viederman on translating strong environmental concern into environmentally sound behavior, Bonnie Shephard on the importance of individual consciousness raising and empowerment, Daniel Goleman on the courage to seek and speak the truth that can save us from the narcotic of self-deception, Brian Wynne on reconstructing ourselves to achieve a sustainable environment, William Keeping on an "ecopsychology" to replace mainstream academic psychology which views humans as distinct from nature, and John E. Mack on "blowing the traditional Western mind" and on a comprehensive psychology of the environment that includes spiritual elements, appreciates our relationship with the Earth, and encourages our reconnection.

**Toward Sustainable Communities: A Resource Book for Municipal and Local Governments.** Mark Roseland (Centre for Human Settlements, University of British Columbia). Ottawa: National Round Table on the Environment and the Economy, December 1992. 340p. free. (613/992-7189). *

Seeks to enable local government officials and citizens to apply the concept of "sustainable development" in their communities, in that enlightened local decisions on environmental issues will be of global as well as local benefit. Chapters discuss the meaning of sustainable development, the city as eco-system, climate change and air quality, transport planning and traffic management, land use and growth management, energy conservation and efficiency, solid and hazardous waste reduction and recycling, water and sewage, edible planting and indigenous landscaping, economic development for a sustainable economy, healthy communities, environmental education, green investment and purchasing, leadership by example, environmental administration, and regional programs. Each chapter includes description of key books, articles, and organizations.

**The United States Goes Green.** (Special Report), Brad Knickerbocker, *The Christian Science Monitor*, Tues, 12 January 1993, 8-13. *

"The environmental movement in the US today stands poised to have greater influence than ever before." There are as many as 10,000 environmental organizations in the US today, ranging from local groups that may exist for only a few months to established institutions with dozens of lawyers, scientists, and economists on their staff. Environmental groups in the past few years have seen steep increases in contributions, largely due to threats from the Reagan and Bush administrations. The 20 largest groups together can now raise $1 billion a year. The National Wildlife Federation (the largest of the so-called "Big 10" environmental groups, with 5.3 million members and supporters) has an annual budget larger than the UN Environmental Programme. Other articles in this report include an interview with Vice President Al Gore Jr. ("who may be characterized as the nation's senior environmentalist"), and profiles of the greening of business, grass-roots activists, and the "wise use" counter movement (much smaller than the environmentalists, but it has won some significant victories). Ron Tipton of the Wilderness Society predicts that "One of the results of the election is that the wise-use movement is going to be bigger and meaner and better financed, now that they have a bogeyman in the White House."

**Valuing The Earth: Economics, Ecology, and Ethics.** Edited by Herman E. Daly and Kenneth Townsend, Cambridge, MA: MIT Press, 1992 . 384pp. $18.95 pb.

*Valuing the Earth* collects more than twenty classic and recent essays that broaden economic thinking by setting the economy in its proper ecological and ethical context. They vividly demonstrate that , contrary to current macroeconomic preoccupations, continued growth on a planet of finite resources cannot be physically or economically sustained. Among the issues addressed are population growth, resource use, pollution, theology (east and west), energy, and economic growth. Their common theme is that an economic steady state is more healthful to life on earth than unlimited growth.

**Visions of a Sustainable World.** *Engineering & Science*, 55:3, Spring 1992. 60p. $2.00 from California Institute of Technology, [Pasadena CA 91125 (818/356-3630)]. *

Highlights of an October 1991 symposium at the California Institute of Technology, dedicated to Harrison Brown (1917-1986), Caltech professor, author of **The Challenge of Man's Future** (Viking, 1954). **Murray Gell-Mann** (Professor of Theoretical Physics and Nobel Laureate) focuses on the key concept of achieving "sustainable quality" and discusses transitions over the next few decades in human population, technology, economic accounting, inter- and intra-generational equity, and ideology. **Harlan Cleveland** (President, World Academy of Art and Science) considers managing human behavior in the global commons (space, the atmosphere, oceans, Antarctica) and the need for a UN Trusteeship Commission to act as trustee for our four great surrounding environments. **Carl Djerassi** (Stanford University) outlines prospects in contraception and proposes rallying cry of "Make abortion unnecessary." **Gregory Benford** (University of California-Irvine) imagines the 21st century as "a biological century" informed by living technology and the demographic explosion. Various panels discuss a sustainable global commons (with special emphasis on biodiversity), development for a sustainable future (requiring a much stronger commitment to equity and social justice than at present), the technological transition to a hydrogen economy, the economic transition to recognizing total costs, the transition to global governance, and cultural and ideological transitions.

**World Resources 1992-93: A Guide to the Global Environment.** World Resources Institute (Allen L. Hammond, Editor-in-Chief), in collaboration with the UN Environment Programme and the UN Development Programme. New York: Oxford University Press, March 1992. 385p. $29.95; $15.95pb. *

Fifth edition of a biennial series, with editions in eight languages. **Part I**, in support of the UNCED meeting, focuses on sustainable development with four special chapters. The overview chapter, providing an extensive definition of sustainable development, concludes that it requires simultaneous progress along at least four dimensions: economic, human, environmental, and technological. The three other chapters provide case studies on what sustainable development might mean in industrial countries, poor countries (breaking the cycle of poverty and environmental degradation), and rapidly industrializing countries. **Part II**, as in previous editions, focuses on a particular region, in this case the severe problems faced by Central Europe. (The fourth edition focusedon Latin America; the third edition on Asia.)

**World Without End: Economics, Environment, and Sustainable Development.** David W. Pearce (University College London) and Jeremy J. Warford (Senior Advisor, Environment Department, The World Bank). Published for the World Bank. New York: Oxford University Press, January 1993. 440p. $39.95. *

If poverty is to be reduced and the standard of living improved, economic growth must remain a legitimate objective of national governments and the world community. Limits can be avoided and the world will not necessarily come to an end - if imaginative policies are devised and implemented. Pursuing economic growth without adequate attention to the environment is not sustainable. The issue is how, not whether, to grow. The causes of much environmental degradation lie in the workings of the economy, and in economic distortions of government policies. The major theme in this book is the need for incentives to conserve resources and to change technology, especially in the poorest countries. Chapters discuss environmental economics, the concept of sustainable development, the choice of discount rate, environmental accounting and indicators, evaluating environmental damage and benefits, population growth and carrying capacity, pricing for cost recovery, market failure, environmental taxes, marketable permits, property rights and resource management (privatization can provide incentives to improve land and resources, but can also lead to degradation and externalities; common property management can work with proper incentives), poverty and the environment, world markets and natural resource degradation, transfrontier environmental issues, and managing global resources. [ALSO SEE: **Economic Policy Towards the Environment**, edited by Dieter Helm of New College, Oxford (Blackwell, Oct 1991. 326p. $24.95), with 11 essays, including David Pearce on saving tropical forests.]

**Note:** * The majority of these annotated references were contributed by or adapted from *The Future Survey*, Michael Marien, ed., a publication of The World Future Society, 7900 Woodmont Avenue, Suite 450, Bethesda, MD 290814. (301) 656-8274. The World Future Society, an association for the study of alternative futures, is a non-profit educational and scientific organization founded in 1966. The Society acts as an impartial clearinghouse for a variety of different views and does not take positions on what will happen — or ought to happen — in the future.

# Other References of Note:

For information on obtaining copies of these works, please contact the World Engineering Partnership for Sustainable Development at (703)750-6401 or via facsimile at (703)750-6506.

Carnegie Commission. *International Environmental Research and Assessment: Proposals for Better Organization and Decision Making.* New York: The Carnegie Commission on Science, Technology, and Government, 1992.

Cherrington, Mark. "Engineers Salvage the Future." *Earthwatch.* May/June 1993, p.16.

Florman, Samuel C. "Engineering and the Concept of Elite." *The Bridge.* Fall 1991.

*Guidelines for Environmental Engineering.* Institution of Engineers, Australia, 1987, 1989, 1991.

Hatch, Henry. "A Design for Sustainable Development." *Engineering Times.* April 1992: p.5.

Hartley, Peter. "Maximum Torque: Or, What is Engineering?" *Mineral & Energy Resources*, Colorado School of Mines. March 1981.

Hofmann, Ernst. "Harmonization Between Man and Environment: Actions for the Profession." International Federation of Consulting Engineers (FIDIC) Annual Conference. Tokyo, Japan, September 1991. Rajagopalan, V. "The Engineers' Role in Sustainable Development." *Civil Engineering.* August 1992: p.6.

Solow, R. M. *Sustainability: An Economist's Perspective.* The Eighteenth J. Seward Johnson Lecture. Woods Hole Oceanographic Institution Marine Policy Center, Woods Hole, MA, June 14, 1991.

Speth, James Gustave. "EPA Must H elp Lead an Environmental Revolution in Technology." *Hazardous Material Control Magazine.* November/December 1991: p. 27.

Tibbs, Hardin. "Industrial Ecology: An Environmental Agenda for Industry." Cambridge, MA: Arthur D. Little, Inc., 1991.

Selected papers of *Transactions of the Institution of Professional Engineers New Zealand*, Vol. 18, 1/GEN. The Institution of Professional Engineers New Zealand. November 1991.

The World Conservation Union (IUCN), United Nations Environment Programme, World Wildlife Fund for Nature, *Caring for the Earth: A Strategy for Sustainable Living*, Gland , Switzerland, October 1991.

Weston, Roy F. *Sustainable Development: The Economic Model of the Future (Role of the Engineering Profession)*. West Chester, PA: Roy F. Weston, Inc., 1992.

Note: *All United Nations publications including the full text of Agenda 21, and the Rio Declaration, can be obtained from* **UN Publications, Sales Section, Room DC2-0853, United Nations, New York City, New York, 10017, USA.** *The text of the Climate and Biodiversity Conventions can be obtained from the* **Project Manager for Sustainable Development, Department of Public Information, Room S-894, United Nations, New York City, New York, 10017, USA.**

# Index of Annotated References

# Sustainable Engineering
## Contact Information

**World Engineering Partnership for Sustainable Development (WEPSD)**
Attn.William Robertson or Monica Ellis
c/o GETF
7010 Little River Turnpike
Suite 290
Annandale, Virginia  22003  USA
Phone: (703)-750-6401
Fax: (703)-750-6506

**American Association of Engineering Societies**
Attn:  Harry Tollerton,
1111 19th Street, N.W., Suite 608
Washington , D.C.  20036-3690
Phone: 202-296-2237
Fax: 202-296-1151.

**World Federation of Engineering Organizations (WFEO)**
Attn: John McKenzie
1-7 Great George Street
London SW10 3AA, England
Phone: 222-7722
Fax: 222-0812.

**International Federation of Consulting Engineers (FIDIC)**
Atttn: Marshall Gysi
FIDIC Secretariat
Avenue du Temple, 13c, Chailly,
CH1012, Lausanne, Switzerland
Phone: 633-5003
Fax: 653-5432

**International Union of Technical Associations (UATI)**
Attn: Pierre Pecoux
Maison de l'UNESCO
1, Rue Miollis
f-75732 Paris Cedex 15 France
Phone: 45-669410
Fax: 43-062927

**Institution of Engineers-Australia (IEAUST)**
Engineering House
11 National Circuit Barton ACT 2600
Australia
Phone (06) 270-6555
Fax: (06) 273-1488.